FRO
CHILDREN

TO

BRETHREN

How do I know when my child
is ready for baptism?

Edited by Bob Whiddon, Jr.

ISBN 1-878579-06-1

S.U.N. Publishing
P.O. Box 381
Westminster, CO 80030
(303) 753-2915

Table of Contents

PREFACE

It scared me to death. I had no idea what to do or what to say. That little red-headed girl had asked me when I was going to let her get baptized. She had gone to Bible classes almost from the day she was born. And I knew that someday she would be baptized into Jesus Christ for the forgiveness of her sins. It was going to be great.

I never thought that day was coming so soon. She's only eleven. How am I supposed to know when she's ready for baptism? For some reason it caught me completely off guard. I was scared to death.

The idea for this book was born out of panic. I found little printed on the specific subject of baptizing children and that "age of accountability." I confided in my fellow preachers in the Denver area for their wisdom and experiences as they had gone through this.

I was so greatly benefited by their wisdom that I felt that the rest of the brotherhood should hear what they had to say. So I asked them to write down what they told me.

Hopefully you can gain much from the discussion in these pages. There are no pat-answers. There are no miracle cures. But there is a lot to think about.

Baptism is the most important decision that anyone can make. My daughter will be baptized, someday, perhaps not soon. But when she does, I'll stand confident that my wife and I helped her as much as we possibly could.

Talking to a child about baptism is not easy. But maybe through the experiences of others, it'll be a little less frightening.

Yours in the struggle
to preach to the children,

Bob Whiddon, Jr.
August 7, 1992

THE AGE OF ACCOUNTABILITY

by Bob Whiddon, Jr.

When is a child able to commit sin? At what point does mischievouseness become unrighteousness? At what point do children understand that the eternal promises of God are more real than the presents left under a tree, inside a house, supposedly by a red-suited man who came in through the chimney?

As we wonder "when" our children ought to be baptized, we often hear the phrase "the age of accountability." Logically, there has to be a point in the life of a child when he will be able to understand the need for repentance, confession, and baptism into Jesus Christ. But when is this age of accountability? When do a child's mistakes become disobedience to the will of God?

What Does Accountability Mean?

The Bible is remarkably silent about the age when a child must put on the Lord in baptism. Even the phrase "age of accountability" is nowhere mentioned in Scripture. However, the Bible is clear with its statements concerning the spiritual position of young children and mature adults. It's the in-between stage that we wonder about.

1

A child cannot inherit sin from his father (Ezekiel 18:4, 20). Jesus taught, *"unless you are converted and become like little children, you shall not enter the kingdom of heaven"* (Matthew 18:4). This verse can mean that we must become humble like a child or teachable like a child. But perhaps its greatest meaning is that we are to be sinless as a child. Since our conversion washes away our sins, we enter the same spiritual position as children—without sin. Children are given to us as representations of true Christianity. So special are these little representatives that Jesus guarded them and rebuked anyone who would cause them to stumble (Mark 13:10ff). Children are sinless. There is nothing in their nature or actions that would cause them to be separated from God.

On the other hand, adults are sinners (Romans 3:23) and sinful actions cause adults to be separated from God (Romans 6:23). The word "sin" in the original language meant to "miss the mark," i.e., to not live up to the purpose that the Lord has set for us. For this reason the gospel message is clear:

"...be baptized...for the forgiveness of sins...." (Acts 2:38)

"Arise and be baptized, and wash away your sins...." (Acts 22:16)

"He who believes and is baptized shall be saved." (Mark 16:16)

These are the two extremes. Children are sinless and do not need baptism. They make mistakes, are mischievous, and sometimes disobedient. But they are not sinners. Adults are sinners and must be baptized in order to be saved. They are responsible or accountable for their actions. If they know the right thing to do and don't do it, it is sin (James 4:17). And if their sin is not forgiven before the Lord comes again, they are lost.

So when is it? When do children grow up enough to become responsible (accountable) for sins? When do they cross the line from innocent to accountable?

What Do They Have To Know To Be Baptized?

Baptism requires understanding. There are many examples of conversion in the Bible showing that understanding is a vital part of baptism.

For the Jews on the Day of Pentecost, they understood the prophecies of Joel and David concerning the future Messiah (Acts 2:16-35). They also understood that their godlessness was responsible for the murder of Jesus, the Son of God (2:23, 36). With this guilt in their heart they asked what they were supposed to do (2:37). Peter told them that baptism would remove those sins for which they were accountable (2:38).

The Philippian Jailer was about to commit suicide when he came to the Lord in baptism. An earthquake had rocked the prison that he was guarding (Acts 16:19ff). The jailer assumed that all of the prisoners had escaped. Knowing that a slow, painful execution awaited a soldier who neglected his duties, the jailer chose the easy way out—suicide. Before he could successfully kill himself, Paul assured him that no prisoner had escaped. The jailer asked, *"What must I do to be saved?"* He was not asking about eternal life in heaven. He was asking how he could escape his torturers. But the answer was the same, *"Believe on the Lord Jesus, you and your house, and you shall be saved."* The jailer received a crash course in who Jesus was, his power, and the washing away of sins through baptism. He and his household were baptized that very night.

The apostle Paul had to have a bit of understanding before his baptism. Paul was zealous in his service to God through the Jewish religion, but he did not understand the prophecies concerning the Messiah, nor did he understand that Jesus was the fulfillment of prophecy. Instead he tried to wipe out the memory of Jesus and his followers. But Paul was blinded by Jesus on the road to Damascus (Acts 9:3ff). Jesus made him understand that his efforts in persecution were hurting Jesus and his plan. Then the preacher, Ananias, came and instructed Paul to be baptized so that his sins might be washed away (Acts 22:16).

All three of these cases have a common thread of understanding on the part of the one being baptized. Not all of them had the same knowledge or background. They were taught, beginning with their present state of mind, enough to know about the saving power of Jesus through baptism.

There must be understanding before baptism. The act of being immersed is an experience of faith. Baptism is an opportunity to call on the name of the Lord (Acts 22:16) and appeal to Him to cleanse the conscience (I Peter 3:21). If a person does not have some understanding of these matters, then his immersion is no different than a young child being pushed under water at the neighborhood swimming pool.

So again we wonder, "When do children get to that point of understanding?" Is this the same as the age of accountability? At age six we can sit down and teach children the story of Jesus. And they may be able to answer questions about baptism. They may even tell us that baptism is to forgive sins. But do they understand—really understand? When are they old enough?

Is Twelve the Magical Age?

There is some feeling that children reach the age of understanding and accountability around age twelve. Where do we come up with this?

Society and the Twelve Year Old

Social Services in many states have chosen age twelve as the age that a child is able to handle limited responsibilities in society. Before this, they say, a child is not able to make responsible decisions.

"By the time kids are 9 or 10, you can train them in safety and talk to them," said Gail Ryan, spokeswoman with the Kemp

Center for Prevention and Treatment of Child abuse. "They have a consciousness of what's safe and they know how to make emergency calls. But you can't leave children alone or caring for younger children until they're 12. Otherwise, (parents) subject themselves to being found guilty of neglect" [1]

After reading the article above, I still wondered why age twelve was picked. I phoned Gail Ryan at her office in Denver. She said that psychological studies over the years have proven that age twelve is the average age when children become "developmentally, morally, and ethically able to make decisions."

I called the Social Services department in the county in which I live. They told me that there was no law concerning how old a child must be before he can be left alone at home. But they added that age twelve was the "rule of thumb" and that each case would evaluated on its own merits.

Public school systems show a different approach in teaching the elementary students (age 12 and under) than the junior high students (over 12 years old). In a phone conversation with Dr. Gonzalo Ramirez, principle and brother-in-law in Lamesa TX, he stated that the change in teaching methods in junior high schools had more to do with the needs of the teachers. There is a need for teachers to specialize in subjects to keep up with the increasing knowledge of students of that age. But when questioned as to why schools begin this new way of teaching at age 12, he replied, "It's tradition more than anything."

Puberty and the Twelve Year Old

Around this same time in life is the awkward stage of puberty. Bodies are changing. Emotions more easily surface. The children are beginning to care how they look to themselves and others.

But not just bodies and emotions are changing. The children are questioning, wondering why things are the way they are. Their abilities to reason are increased. Abstract concepts are more understandable.

God, heaven, and baptism are abstract concepts. A younger child may know the right answers to biblical questions. But until they reach that age, somewhere around puberty, they may not really understand.

Pubescent children begin to ask questions about God and if He really is there. The idea of washing away of invisible sins in a non-magical pool of water now begins to make a little sense.

The age of puberty is a confusing yet eye-opening time of life. And it so happens that the average (?) age is somewhere around twelve.

Traditions and the Twelve Year Old

The religious world places great importance on the change in children around age twelve. Have you ever wondered why the only story in the Bible of Jesus growing up was when He was twelve years old? According to tradition when a boy reached the age of twelve he began his life's work at the side of his father.[2] If his father was a shepherd, he began shepherding at age twelve. If his father was a carpenter, he would begin his work then at the shop. Jesus, knowing He was the Son of God, assumed that he needed to be "in his Father's house" (Luke 2:49) at age twelve.

The Jews later added a tradition of bar mitzvah (son of the law) for 13 year old boys. This may correspond to the teachings of the Mishnah.

A girl who is 11 years old plus one day may make a vow, but her vow must be examined whether she knew the nature of the vow. When she is twelve years old plus one day her vows are valid.

A boy who is 12 years old plus one day may make a vow,

but his vow must be examined whether he knew the nature of the vow. When he is 13 years old plus one day his vows are valid. (Niddah 5:6)

The Catholic church has three main sacraments related to the children. The first is baptism of an infant where the parents make the decision for them. The second is First Communion which takes place around second grade or seven years old. The third sacrament is Confirmation. This is when the child is old enough to confirm that he now stands as a child of God on his own initiative rather than on his parents' decision. For many Catholic churches, confirmation begins around age twelve though some are waiting until the later teen years.

Denominational traditions, whether good or bad, place emphasis on the child around this certain age. Could these kinds of tradition have influenced the churches of Christ to pick this age as the allusive "age of accountability?"

Statistics and the Twelve Year Old

Dr. Flavil Yeakley, Jr. did some research into baptism and children.[3] He found that statistically the age of twelve was the dividing line in many areas. If a person was baptized before age twelve he was more likely to fall away from the church or get re-baptized than those baptized after age twelve. In fact, he found that only 2% of those baptized before age ten remained faithful or were satisfied with their original baptism. Dr. Yeakley attributes these amazing facts to the ability of children (around age twelve) to begin thinking abstractly. He also found that the longer the child waited to be baptized, in the later teen years, the more likely he would remain faithful.

Conclusion

It is evident that major changes go on in the life of the child around the age of twelve. It is evident that the average twelve year old can begin to understand abstracts concepts such as sin, baptism, commitment, Lordship of Jesus, etc. But perhaps we should emphasize the word "begin."

Should we say that twelve is the age of accountability? No. We could say that it is the age when children begin to understand accountability. I am not advocating baptizing all children at age twelve nor am I saying that all children should wait until their later teen years. The Bible is remarkably silent about this matter. God apparently allows us to use our own wisdom, feelings, and experiences to know when the right time is for our child's baptism.

Keep reading this book. Consider the information in the following chapters. And pray a lot for wisdom as you work with your children.

One last thing. There is a story in the Bible that comes close to defining an age of accountability. When Israel gained its freedom from Egypt it began to prepare itself for war. Men of war were those twenty years old and older (Numbers 1:3). When God became angry at their faithlessness, he forced them to wander in the wilderness for 40 years until all those men of war had died (Deuteronomy 2:14, 16). But if they were under twenty years old at the time of God's anger, they were not accountable for the sins of the people. They were even called *"little ones...who have no knowledge of good and evil"* (Deuteronomy 1:39). You see, up through age 19 they were not accountable. But twenty year olds were accountable. Something to think about!

---

[1] Tillie Fong and Charlene Chu, "Are they ready to be home alone?" (Rocky Mountain News, June 14, 1992) p. 14.

[2] Anthony Lee Ash, The Gospel According to Luke Part I, 1:1-9:50 (Sweet Publishing Company: Austin, Texas, 1972), p. 64.

[3] Flavil R. Yeakley, Jr., Why Churches Grow (Nashville, Tenn: Christian Communications, Inc., 1979) pp., 26-31.

IT ALL BEGINS AT THE CRADLE

by Don Canter

The parents' first view of the baby is not the best one! The color is bad! There's "stuff" covering the body which must be removed! The cry is annoying! However, those first glimpses may be the most exciting and memorable. We can't wait to get our hands on him.!

Once a baby is cleaned and presented, parents find themselves in a state of pure ecstasy! All the hours of waiting and discomfort are forgotten! The pain of labor slips into virtual obscurity! We are ready to enjoy God's precious gift! We marvel at God's handiwork.

After a few days' stay in the hospital, baby is taken home. What a beautiful picture as baby is placed in the well prepared and decorated room! That cradle (crib), empty for so long, now holds the most beautiful and precious baby the world has ever seen! That's because it's ours! Our dream is realized!

The Reality of It

Then reality strikes! We realize that a soul headed for eternity is entrusted to our care! We, as parents, are charged with the sobering responsibility of bringing that child *"up in the nurture*

9

and admonition of the Lord" (Ephesians 6:4). Prayer is needed! We pray, "Lord, give us wisdom and strength for the task. We beseech your help and guidance. We want to be the best parents possible but recognize our own inabilities. Lord, heaven is our goal for this child, and we plead for your intervention and activity to make that a reality." Yes, the time to begin on our knees in behalf of our new baby is when that child is in the cradle! To delay is detrimental! Not to pray is presumptuous.

To underscore the need to point our children in the direction of Christ and Christianity at an extremely early age, Dr. Maria Montessori (and others) emphasize the fact that a child learns as much in the first three years as an adult does in 60.[1] "By the age of three, the child has already laid down the foundation of his personality as a human being."[2] Conscientious and informed Christian parents will be cognizant of the fact that the waste of early years of training opportunities can never be compensated! Research clearly bears out the truth that the most important years of life for training purposes are not university years but the first six. An unmistakable truth must be reckoned with: the first few years of life affect all the rest.

Illustration

Those who believe in Christian education at the university level will begin early to orient their children. Reinforcements will come frequently. We may say things like, "When you get to the Christianity University you will meet all kinds of neat people. You will make lasting friends." Parents are very much aware that if they begin planting the seeds for a Christian education in elementary school rather than springing the thought on their children when they are high school seniors, the dream and expectation is enhanced.

The same principle is true regarding our children becoming Christians. If we can begin in the earliest of formative years extolling the virtues of Christianity and the beauty of a life in

Christ, the potential of their dying to sin and being buried with Christ in baptism is strengthened. If we say nothing regarding a new life in Christ during those early years and suddenly spring on them the need to surrender they may rebel.

When to Teach

A favorite question of Christian parents is, "When do I teach my child about baptism?" Answer: from the cradle! No, you may not mention the term baptism, but all the times of sharing with them the love of God, speaking to them about loving and obeying God, following God, being like Christ, etc., you are sharing instruction about baptism on the basic level.

While Deuteronomy 6:4-9 has been a "catch-all" passage for teaching children, it certainly has application regarding when to teach. Note the text:

"Hear, O Israel; the Lord our God is one Lord; and thou shalt love the Lord thy God with all thine heart, and with all thy soul, and with all thy might. And these words, which I command thee this day, shall be in thine heart; and thou shalt teach them diligently unto thy children, and shall talk of them when thou sittest in thine house, and when thou walkest by the way, and when thou liest down, and when thou risest up. And thou shalt bind them for a sign upon thine hand, and they shall be as frontlets between thine eyes. And thou shalt write them upon the posts of thy house and on thy gates."

God pleads with Israel to love the Lord with all their hearts. The words He has taught them are to be taught diligently to their children when they sit in the house, when taking walks, when lying down, when they get up, and they are to post those words all around the house. There needs to be constant reminders at every juncture in the lives of our children that there really is one Lord. It is virtually impossible to plant and provoke too many subtle thoughts!

11

This gives us a clear indication that teaching is to take place in every mode of life. No situation is exempt! Teaching that leads to the baptism of our children will be a natural expression of our faith no matter where we are. Rather than focusing on the "perfect opportunity," focus on all the opportunities!

There is an important ingredient in this teaching process; it is parents! Mothers and fathers are to be devoted role models for their children. Role models teach! Role models exemplify what they teach! If the model is faulty, the message is distorted!

How to Teach

Methodology may be all important or irrelevant depending on the situation. At times a strong defense of a doctrine is enhanced by a structured presentation. On other occasions, the need to teach is best met by statements of conviction from scripture without a long dissertation. In other words, be flexible. If the situation calls for an extended discussion, do it! If the need can best be served by casually offering suggestions, do it! There are teachable moments every day in addition to structured times. We capitalize on convenient times and create others by being conscious of the need to communicate God's eternal message!

Three suggestions loom large; (1) **Be informed**. In molding our children there is a compelling need to be informed and able to recognize such things as evolution, humanism, and agnosticism. Good materials are available. It behooves us to secure and read them. We must not fear any challenge to truth. Truth will triumph! Our basic problem is generating enough self-discipline to discover truth! (2) **Be willing to confront**. A passive attitude is destructive. If a topic needs to be addressed, do so! The philosophy "it will work itself out" or "it will all come out in the wash" is false and fatalistic. Solomon recorded, "The child left to himself will bring his mother to shame" (Proverbs 29:15). Education rather than evasion is the answer! (3) **A sincere love for the child**. We are very much aware of the studies which have indicated that a child cannot survive without tender loving care. Love for our children simply suggests that we are aware of the importance of the child as an individual, that the child has certain identifiable needs, and we are interested in what is best for the child. One of the reasons God made families is to provide an atmosphere where children can be loved and their needs could be met. Children need the continuing influence of a mother and father. How then do we teach? Through love, i.e., seeking and serving their best interests! Obviously, if there is no love there will be no teaching! To fail to teach is to fail our children! By refusing or neglecting to teach our children we are robbing them of the most important thing we have to offer as parents! It's the one thing which will last. David said, *"Thy word have I hid in mine heart, that I might not sin against thee"* (Psalm 119:11). Parents have the awesome responsibility of hiding (planting) God's word in the hearts of their children!

What to Teach

From the cradle, children can be taught. If we don't believe it, we must visit some "cradle roll" classes which are well developed. True, they aren't able to grasp such things as plenary verbal inspiration, but they can begin to learn about creation and that God is a God of love. Such a vital message must be communicated early! To delay is to waste time and opportunities which cannot be recaptured!

Some truths need to be instilled in our children from birth. Among the most obvious of those would be the love and security found in their parents, that there is a God who wonderfully and marvelously made all that surrounds us, that the church is God's institution and vitally important, and consistency and commitment to learning about God and His love are invaluable to our welfare. Parents must make sure their children are exposed to these truths "from birth!"

It's interesting how much children learn from their parents. That's why it is so critical that we be a model of devotion and faithfulness. When discussing what to teach from the cradle, it is paramount that we include the importance of parental example and modeling. Note the following: (1) When parents demonstrate a tremendously vibrant faith, the same is instilled in the child. We are naive to think that parents can give every indication of doubt regarding whether or not God really notices us, whether or not God is really active in the affairs of our world, whether or not salvation is real or just a figment of our imagination, and whether or not God really calls us to faithfulness, and then expect the child to really trust in God! (2) When parents fully exemplify the love of God in dealing with others, children develop the same trait. Yet, when parents speak disparagingly of others, are unkind towards brothers and sisters, bear grudges, etc., children become confused. Parents must demonstrate a love for God and others in the presence of their children from the cradle! (3) When parents truly put God first (Matthew 6:33), children are taught a most vital lesson. However, when parents vacillate between loving the world and honoring God (I John 2:15-17), children obviously get a mixed message. Parents must love the Lord God with all their heart, soul, and mind all the time.

It may sound rather trite and trivial but it is true: what we share academically will have little impact on our children unless it is modeled and reinforced by a conscientious, consistent Christian lifestyle.

Conclusion

When should I begin teaching my child about commitment and baptism? Emphatically, from the cradle! A well-planned strategy and curricula for training a child must be initiated just after birth! Lessons can be taught from the earliest days of childhood. Simple lessons taught to saturation rather than sporadically build faith! Regular reminders are required (II Timothy 2:14; II Peter 1:12; Jude 5). This practice helps insulate the child against departing "from the training received as a child" (Proverbs 22:16). When I follow the regimen—I will teach my child wherever I am, whatever I'm doing, whenever I can, and whoever might be present—and from the cradle, I will help solidify my child's faith in the Lord God! This structure will be so engaging that our children will be led to obey *"from the heart that form of doctrine which was delivered"* (Romans 6:17) resulting in salvation! Likewise, that obedience will be so meaningful that they will *"continue in the Son, and in the Father"* (I John 2:24).

Joy will be the result when we accept responsibility for teaching our children even while "rocking the cradle."

[1] Maria Montessori, The Absorbent Mind, (New York, New York, Dell Publishing Company, Inc., 1967) p. 7.
[2] Ibid., p. 8.

COMMITMENT IN BAPTISM

by Russ Cole

Baptism is always presented in scripture as an act of commitment to Jesus Christ. It was not entered into lightly, or because "everyone else was doing it," or because it seemed like the right thing to do at the moment. Baptism is an act of contrition and consecration resulting in a definitive change of life.

Romans 6 presents this picture as clearly as any passage. Somehow these Roman Christians to whom Paul was writing had come to believe that a sinful lifestyle was acceptable because God's grace would cover them.

On the contrary Paul writes, *"May it never be!"* He then reminds them of what took place at their baptism.

"We died to sin, how can we live in it any longer? Or don't you know that all of us who were baptized into Jesus Christ were baptized into his death? We were therefore buried with him through baptism into death in order that, just as Christ was raised from the dead through the glory of the Father, we too may live a new life." (Romans 6:2-4)

Two words in these verses represent the heart of Paul's message: death and life. In baptism the old life of sin is crucified with him" (vs. 6). Christians are in effect "dead to sin" (vs. 11). Following the experience of death and burial there is a resurrection in which Christians are raised to live a *new life*.

A major feature of this new life is its change of masters. Whereas before baptism our lives are under the control of sin, after baptism we are subjects of Jesus Christ. Therefore, sin is not to reign in our mortal bodies (vs. 12). We are *"dead to sin, but alive to God in Christ Jesus"* (vs. 11). By the power of God we have been taken from death to life, from old self to new self. A transformation has occurred. Paul does not use the term in Romans 6, but the necessity of "commitment" rings loud and clear. In baptism we commit to a new master. We vow to put away those things that do not please our Lord.

F. LaGard Smith emphasizes the commitment involved in baptism by comparing it to marriage, with baptism being the wedding ceremony.[1] Couples who marry commit to each for life. They promise to love, honor, obey, and be faithful unto death. Because of their commitment and love, they seek to do that which pleases and helps the other. They often grow to like the same foods, entertainment, activities, and friends. Their dislikes become similar as well.

In the same way, when we commit to Christ we vow to love, honor, obey, and be faithful unto death. We promise to submit ourselves to his leadership and obey only his desires. In time we grow to be more and more like him, hating what he hates and loving what he loves.

It is in baptism that our vow to serve Christ is consummated and our new life under his lordship is begun. We no longer live as we did before. We live now as the "bride" of Jesus Christ. Baptism is, as Smith puts it, *"the believer's wedding ceremony."*

In light of the commitment involved in baptism, how are

we to know when our own children are ready to take this important step? Like most Christian parents, my wife and I struggle with this question. We have three children, all of whom we pray will be faithful, committed children of God. We want their faith to be personal, genuine, and vibrant. We want them to have the mind, spirit, and heart of Jesus Christ. Does the realization of these desires relate in any way to the age at which our children are baptized? I believe it does.

While God never put an age on baptism, he did not leave us in the dark about what is required. No doubt a genuine commitment to Jesus is essential. Every new believer will grow in his understanding of commitment as they mature in Christ. But an initial commitment is critical to the conversion experience.

As already stated, commitment involves a moral consciousness of one's own sinfulness. It also requires surrender to the will of God, who graciously provided for us a way of life in the face of certain death. It is grace understood and grace taken seriously.

A simple illustration might help. As parents we know how much more our children appreciate those items they work toward and pay for with their own money. My first car never had it so good! Why? Because I paid for it in cash from my own life-savings. I knew what it cost me.

Commitment stems from knowing what our salvation cost God. *"You were bought with a price,"* says Paul (I Corinthians 6:20). That price was the blood of Jesus, shed for our sin (Romans 5:6-11). It's on the basis of this price that Paul can say, *"therefore, honor God with your body."* In this context, personal holiness is the result of comprehending the dreadful consequences of our sin and the amazing grace of God.

At what age does a child begin to understand that kind of commitment? It is one thing to admit to sin. It is entirely another to understand the enormous spiritual consequences of sin. The horror of realizing the enormity of their sinfulness caused the Jews on Pentecost to cry out, *"What shall we do?"* (Acts 2:37). In response to God's gracious provision of salvation, three thousand of them committed their lives to Christ in baptism that very day (Acts 2:41). Does it not seem important that our own children understand what it cost God to provide a way of salvation for them?

I believe there is a tendency for the children of Christian families to miss the significance of this kind of commitment. The reality of sin fails to hit home because they have been immersed in Christianity all their lives. In a sense they come to Christ with their goodness, not with their sin. They unconsciously adopt a meritorious-works perspective of salvation, believing heaven is deserved.

Consequently, many baptized young people do not experience conversion, at least not at their baptism. Many of them fall away from the church or drift into apathy. Others become legalistic, continuing to believe that salvation is earned by how "good" they are or by the number of works they can do.

Studies done in the Church of Christ indicate a serious lack of sustained commitment among our young people. In a 1979 survey, Dr. Flavil R. Yeakley, Jr. found that "only 10% of those who were baptized before the age of twelve remained faithful or were satisfied with their original baptism. Even for those who were baptized at the age of twelve, only 44% remained faithful church members."[2] This study counted only those who continued to attend church services. We can only surmise that the percentage of those who could be described as truly committed to Christ would be somewhat smaller.

More recent studies indicate a similar problem. A 1991 survey by David Lewis and Carley Dodd of 3000 young people in the Church of Christ reveals a waning of enthusiasm and excitement for Christ with each passing year after a teen's baptism. They discovered that young people who have grown up in the church see baptism as primarily a "rite of passage," instead of a turning away from sin and turning to Christ. Of those surveyed, the average age of baptism was 12.4 years.[3]

Something is obviously wrong with the approach we have taken to the training and baptism of our youth. Many are coming to the waters of baptism uninformed and unprepared for the kind of commitment required. Should we be surprised that Christ means so little as they grow older? It would seem that our whole philosophy of conversion deserves closer scrutiny.

Whatever else it may be, baptism ought to be part of a conscious, well-considered conversion experience. Anything less than that permits a person to claim false security in an act that, in Scripture, is tied to informed participation and deep personal commitment. Anything less than that fills the church with those who wear the right label, but who don't appreciate what it means to become a new person in Jesus Christ.
Baptism ought to be the greatest of all sacred rites. Instead, doctrinally-misunderstood and wrongly-administered baptism has quietly and methodically been snuffing out the life of the church.[4]

Unquestionably, there are many faithful, dedicated believers who were baptized at a young age. But statistics and personal observance reveal the sobering fact that many others who were baptized in their early youth had no understanding of true commitment to Christ. Their lives and lack of true relationship with Jesus reveal the truth, *"he who has been forgiven little loves little"* (Luke 7:47). They love little because they have never come to appreciate the price paid for their sins. As Bill Love writes, "Unless we tell people what their problem is, grace has no meaning...how do you get the joy of remission unless you know of the cancer?"[5]

Commitment is the fruit of knowing our sinfulness, sensing our helplessness, and finding in Christ our only blessedness. Those converted to Christ in scripture understood this trilogy. From Pentecost to Philippi and beyond, men and women were brought to Christ because they saw in him their only hope. And with these faithful servants God "turned the world upside down." Their commitment did not flinch, even in the fires of persecution.

How can parents help their children understand the meaning of commitment and thus be prepared for their baptism? First and most importantly, we must teach our children to love Jesus Christ more than all. We must model before them what this love means. Spiritual discussions should find their way into everyday conversations and situations. We must help them discover a Lord who died in their place and lives to give them life. We must communicate to them the love of God both in word and in practice. The church can assist the home by emphasizing the relationship behind the rules.

Second, we must not consciously or unconsciously pressure our children to be baptized before they are personally prepared to make such an important commitment. Parents may worry that something is wrong with their child if they are not baptized at some point near an accepted "age of accountability." Yet, we also understand that children mature at different ages. The ability of one child to comprehend the meaning of personal commitment does not mean that other children of similar age are prepared to do the same. The age of accountability varies considerably from one child to another. We must learn to entrust our children to God's grace and pray for His guidance until they are ready to surrender their lives to Christ.

It may help us to be patient if we once again compare baptism to marriage. Not many parents would want their child to marry as a pre-teen or early adolescent! We recognize the serious, life-long commitment involved in marriage and the maturity required of such a union. Baptism is a commitment more important than even that of marriage. Like marriage, it requires a level of maturity and understanding uncommon to many young people in their pre-teen and early adolescent years.[6]

In addition to modeling Christianity and being patient, parents can also help their children by teaching them the true meaning of baptism. As the culmination of the conversion experience, baptism is the ultimate symbol of Christian commitment. It not only marks the beginning of the "new life," it also puts the seal of death on the old. It says to the individual, the church, and to the world, "I have decided to follow Jesus." It is a commitment to sacrifice even life itself for the cause of Christ. To baptize someone who does not or cannot personally comprehend this initial commitment is to deny them the assurance and joy of true conversion and to rob the church of vitality and life.

Personal faith! That is the crying need of the church. A knowing faith! That is what sustains. Baptism is reserved for adults or responsible young people for good reasons. It cannot be overstated that what is at stake is a mature, reflective conversion experience that allows a person to know why he is a Christian and why he has consciously chosen to submit his life to Christ. There are literally millions of people in the world who are Christians in name only. They are "Christians" only because their parents happen to be "Christians" and had them "baptized" in a "Christian" church.[7]

Unfortunately, these "name only" Christians are killing the church. Perhaps the place to begin correcting the problem is with our doctrine of baptism. Instead of fearing that we might loose our children if they are not baptized at a young age, we should honestly face the reality that 44% of those who are baptized end up leaving anyway. Many who do remain in the church are not really converted in heart.

The answer is not simply in the act of baptism, but in the commitment required. If we teach our children to love God with

22

all their hearts, to know what it cost God to save them, and to comprehend the cost of discipleship, then their baptism will represent a true conversion experience.

We will need to wait patiently and prayerfully on the Lord and trust in His grace until the time of their decision. But when that special moment comes, when we witness the new birth of our son or daughter, it will be just that, a *new birth*.

[1] F. LaGard Smith, Baptism: The Believer's Wedding Ceremony (Cincinnati, Ohio: Standard Publishing, 1989)

[2] Flavil R. Yeakley, Jr., Why Churches Grow (Nashville, Tenn.: Christian Communications, Inc., 1979). As reported in Smith, Baptism: The Believer's Wedding Ceremony, p. 162.

[3] Michelle Morris, "Research on Adolescent Spirituality Examines Teen attitudes Toward Christ." (Christian Chronicle, April, 1992.)

[4] Smith, Baptism, p. 163.

[5] Bill Love, as quoted by Roger Massey in Directions in Ministry Vol. 1 no. 2 (Summer, 1992)

[6] See pertinent comments by Smith, Baptism, pp. 152, 154.

[7] Smith, Baptism, p. 165.

"IF I SHOULD DIE BEFORE I WAKE..."

By Gus White III

Of major concern in the issue of the salvation of our children and especially the question of when it is appropriate for them to be baptized into Christ, is the matter of their consciousness of sin and the resulting eternal lostness, and their understanding of faith and obedience and the resulting eternal salvation. Do they understand sin and its consequences? Do they know that they are lost? Do they understand that they can be saved—and how? These are more than academic questions for parents who are trying to guide their children into a faithful relationship with God.

I suppose at one time or another most children hear, and perhaps learn to say, the prayer from the New England Primer, 1777 ed. (the first notice of this prayer is in "Enchiridion Leonis," 1160);

> Now I lay me down to sleep,
> I pray the Lord my soul to keep;
> If I should die before I wake
> I pray the Lord my soul to take.

"If I should die...?" I suspect that most children learn to say those words long before they understand them. Perhaps they

24

carry some meaning of comfort and protection in a child's mind, but certainly not the more mature understanding of being lost or saved when one dies.

When we talk about baptizing children, we are dealing with a much deeper question than their understanding of a church practice.

The Question of the Nature of Baptism

In the question of when our children should be baptized there resides the deeper question of what is involved in baptism in the first place. My children learned at a very early age that in churches of Christ, being baptized was the "thing to do." They knew about being baptized long before they knew about sin and condemnation and the need for salvation. After all, they had heard daddy preach on the subject since their birth, and probably more often than they wanted to hear about it.

There came a day when our oldest boy, who was six years old, and his younger brother, who was almost five, came to me and said, "Daddy, we want to be baptized." I asked, "Why?" They answered, "Because God wants us to be baptized." They clearly understood the church's teaching on the subject. Then I asked what I consider to be the heart of the issue with our children. "Boys, if you were to die right now, would you go to heaven or would you go to hell?" Without hesitation they said, "We would go to heaven!" Of course five and six year old children who have had any teaching at all believe they are going to heaven (and they are). They did not understand sin and its consequences, therefore they could not understand repentance, baptism and salvation. I did not baptize them for another eight years, at which time they came to me and said, "Dad, we need to be baptized because if we are not we are going to be lost." They understood.

The nature of baptism, as explained by Paul in Romans 6, is a spiritual transformation (death, burial, and resurrection with

Christ) effected by God in response to our "informed" faith in the act of atonement. Belief is required (Mark 16:16), and belief requires knowledge of God and His word on the subject. Repentance is required (Acts 2:38), and repentance requires an understanding of sin and lostness. Therefore, I would conclude that before our children are baptized they must come to that point in their lives when they have some understanding of sin, being lost, Christ's sacrifice, God's grace, forgiveness and eternal salvation. In other words, they must come to the point when they fully understand the words, *"If I should die before I wake I pray the Lord my soul to take."*

Christian Camp Experiences

If you have worked with children in a summer Christian camp setting, you have come face to face with the issue of baptizing children. Camp settings are sometimes emotionally charged and the pressures to "get baptized" can be enormous on a young mind not able to rationally reason through the meaning and commitment of baptism.

I remember a summer at camp when two young teens were baptized the second day. They "caught on fire for Jesus" and were thoroughly convinced that it was their God-given commission to baptize every child in camp before the week was over. One of the boys was named Joe, and he became so enthusiastic in his evangelism among the young children that they started to call him "Holy Joe." The third night of the camp session was one I shall never forget. Every ten year old child in the camp was in tears, completely convinced (by "Holy Joe") that the devil would have their soul that very night unless they "got baptized." The children did not even begin to understand what baptism was about, but they were convinced that something terrible was going to happen to them. It took the whole staff, numerous phone calls to parents, and several hours to calm the situation.

The point of this illustration is to say that children can be

26

"made" to be baptized. Parents or teachers can convince the little children there is something very important they need to do to please God. But little children can also be made to brush their teeth, go to school, wash behind their ears, eat their vegies, etc. What we are dealing with here is not whether we can convince the children to be baptized, but whether or not they understand the commitment and the meaning involved in baptism.

A New Testament View

In a study of the subject of baptism in the New Testament it becomes very clear that those who were told to be baptized, or those who were taught about baptism, had some degree of understanding. They understood the meanings and implications of one's own sinfulness and one's personal participation in the death, burial, and resurrection of Jesus in baptism (Acts 2:38; 8:36; 10:47-48; 16:13; Romans 6:3ff).

One of the tendencies in dealing with this subject is to impose a "Jewish" model on modern times. The age of twelve among young Jewish males in Old Testament times, and in the time of Jesus, was significant in that it marked the boundary between childhood and manhood. Remember Jesus' activities in the temple at the age of twelve (Luke 2:41ff)? It is a false assumption to believe that this text, or another text, is to be taken as a model for our times to indicate the age of baptism. There is nothing magic about the age of twelve, and besides, what about the young ladies? The Jews had no such tradition for girls, yet we would not deny a young lady baptism on the basis of the Jewish model.

Again, the important point is one's understanding of the concepts of sin, sinfulness, condemnation, lostness, forgiveness, grace, eternal reward, and commitment of life.

Practical Matters

As the father of three, I can testify that there will be times early in a child's life, especially those being raised in a Christian home, when questions will arise and direction and comfort must be given. As a child grows there is a deepening awareness of God, and then an awful awareness that God condemns the ungodly (an awareness usually gained from Bible classes or from hearing sermons). Sooner or later a child will worry about the things they have done that are wrong, and comfort needs to be given by the parents. But such times at a young age do not necessarily signal the need for baptism. If these times are handled in a sensitive manner, and if you know your child, you need not fear discouraging the child permanently. The question of baptism will arise again.

I believe the need for baptism comes when a young person is so convicted by God's message of sin and condemnation, coupled with His message of grace and salvation, that there is a clear, intelligent decision made to follow God with one's life. Concepts of eternal punishment and eternal reward need to be clearly in place in the youth's mind before the decision to follow (be baptized) can be made. Parents need to be sensitive to such times and not fear saying "yes" too soon.

Practically, parents have a great responsibility in this whole matter. A child's earliest understanding of authority and the concepts of right and wrong come from the parents. It is of eternal importance that parents teach a child from an early age the meaning of having to be responsible to an authority for decisions that are right or wrong.

Concepts of reward and punishment are quite naturally involved in this process. As the child grows, those concepts will evolve into "eternal" concepts. When a child begins to understand the "eternal" nature of things, he begins to understand the afore mentioned concepts of sin, etc. It is then that a child can make a personal decision, not a decision made for him by parents.

Understanding the importance of all this places a great

burden of responsibility upon parents, and well it should. This is not something to be taken lightly. In fact, this matter of the eternal salvation of our children should be "priority one!" This is more important than education, social development, sports, the arts, or any other endeavor our children may pursue with our support and encouragement. It is absolutely essential that we as parents first understand the eternal nature of reward and punishment in our own lives. Nothing is quite as powerful as a living example of an eternal concept. The faithfulness and submission of parents to God's authority speaks more to the children than all the sermons and Bible classes combined. Don't just teach the child, show the child what it means to love God and to be obedient to the heavenly Father. Let them see in you a deep concern for your own soul, a solid understanding of lostness and salvation. If you do, when it comes time to discuss with them the need for their own baptism, the conversation will be much easier and will make a great deal more sense.

A recent survey among churches of Christ has shown that "Teaching and modeling lordship works much better than a rule-oriented approach" in raising our children to be faithful, and that "Parents who openly express their love for God also tend to produce children who are more willing to accept Jesus' lordship."[1] This is the heart of the issue. We do not just want to put our children in the waters of baptism, or to just encourage them to follow a time-honored church tradition. We want them to become disciples of Jesus. When they do, baptism will be a natural result of their desire to let Him be Lord. If we know when they become disciples, we will easily know when they are ready to be baptized.

Conclusion

Perhaps we can change the prayer somewhat to say it from the parent's viewpoint...

Now I lay me down to rest,
I pray the Lord my children's best;

If they should die before they wake
I pray the Lord their soul to take.

Their salvation must be our heart's desire. Their salvation must be our greatest concern. And if it is, I am confident that God will bless each faithful parent with the wisdom needed in encouraging discipleship in their children and in knowing when they need to be baptized.

[1] "Youth Conference: The Many Faces of Christ," an interview of Dr. Carley Dodd and Dr. David Lewis, by Darryl Tippens, in Directions in Ministry, Summer 1992, Vol. 1, no. 2, p. 1.

THE NEED TO UNDERSTAND SIN

by Harold Turner

Most parents, at some time or other, ask, "How old should my child be before being baptized?" Surely no true Christian would want their child to be lost any longer than possible. But the exact age that a child is ready for baptism is not so easily known. Occasionally we hear of a child being baptized at the age of seven years. No doubt some have been baptized at a younger age than seven. Is a child capable of sin at this early age? Does a child, six or seven years old, understand what sin is? Can a child at this age understand what baptism is, and why they are being baptized? Does it make any difference whether or not they understand sin, baptism, and its purpose? These are questions and concerns to parents who want their children to do the right things.

As we consider the need to understand sin before being baptized, let us first observe that the Bible clearly teaches that children are not born lost in sin. Children do not inherit the sins of their parents. Would God, who wants all to be saved (I Timothy 2:4), hold a baby responsible for the conduct of the parents? In Ezekiel 18:14-17 this matter is considered. Ezekiel stated that if the child did not follow his father to do evil, *"He shall not die for the iniquity of his father, he shall surely live."* In verse 19 the people questioned, *"Why does not the son bear the iniquity of the father?"* Ezekiel then answered, *"The soul that sins, it shall die.*

31

The son shall not bear the iniquity of the father, neither shall the father bear the iniquity of the son: the righteousness of the righteous shall be upon him, and the wickedness of the wicked shall be upon him." The wickedness of the wicked will not be upon the righteous, nor will the righteousness of the righteous be upon the wicked. Each person is responsible for his own sins. Jesus compared little children to the kingdom of God (Matthew 18:1-3; 19:14). In Romans 14:17, Paul said the kingdom is righteousness. Thus, we would conclude that children are born righteous.

In Psalm 58:3, the writer stated, *"The wicked are estranged from the womb: they go astray as soon as they be born, speaking lies."* This does not teach that babies are born wicked, or astray, but that they go astray, and that they go astray by speaking lies. Lying originates in the heart from the intent to deceive or mislead another. Until a child reaches the age of planning in the heart to deceive another, they have not gone astray by speaking lies. So, children are not born lost, but do go astray.

At what age do children go astray, and thereby become lost? It is sin that separates the soul from God. Until the child sins, they are pure and in the right relationship with God. To better determine the age when a child sins, we must consider some things about sin.

Sin may be expressed or committed in numerous ways, but sin begins in the heart and grows into wrong thoughts, words, or acts. In I John 3:4, the Bible states, *"Whomsoever commits sin transgresses also the law; for sin is the transgression of the law."* The word "also" indicates that sin takes place before, and is the cause of, the transgression. Jesus taught this to be the case in Mark 7:21-22. *"For from within, out of the heart of men, proceed evil thoughts, adulteries, fornications, murders, thefts, covetousness, wickedness, deceit, lasciviousness, an evil eye, blasphemy, pride, foolishness: all these evil things come from within, and defile the man."* Before any of these evil thoughts, words, or deeds are committed, they are first formed in the heart. Until a child reaches the age of formulating evil in the heart, they are not guilty of sin.

James 1:14-15 shows that sin is a response to lust. *"But every man is tempted, when he is drawn away of his own lust, and enticed. Then when lust has conceived, it brings forth sin: and sin, when it is finished, brings forth death."* Is this lust "fleshly lust", and at what age does a child become influenced by this lust? This is a difficult question to answer. Perhaps it is not until they reach the age of puberty when they begin to change from childhood to adulthood. If so, this would place the age between twelve and fourteen. There is no set rule when this takes place, and this is not to say that there is no type of lust that occurs prior to this point in life. But fleshly lust certainly becomes more acute and sensitive at and following this point of their life.

As parents, we are responsible to teach our children about sin and their response to God, yet with care that we do not encourage them to be baptized before they understand what they are doing. As we teach them right from wrong the child will learn to respond, but not necessarily because they understand what makes their words or acts right or wrong. They learn to respond to certain teachings because of the rewards or punishment occurred by failing to respond properly. When the child fails to respond properly, does this mean they have at that point and time sinned? Not necessarily. For example, we may teach an animal to respond to certain things by reward and punishment. The animal responds, not because they understand, but because of the results. When the animal fails to respond properly, does this mean that the animal sinned? Sin does involve some degree of understanding. James 4:17 says, *"Therefore to him that knows to do good, and does it not, to him it is sin."* This indicates two things—first, the knowledge of what is good, and second, the personal choice to either do or not do it.

Sometimes parents teach their children that certain things

are wrong, but fail to teach why whey are wrong. For example, many times parents have told their children that dancing is a sin, and never teach them why, or what is involved that may make this sin. Is the act, within itself, a sin? It would be difficult to prove that it is. What children need to be taught, and learn, is what causes this to be a danger to their spiritual life. In this case, there may be the lust, the wrong influence, how this might affect another, etc., to consider. If we only teach that acts are what constitute sin, and fail to show why these things involve sin, we are failing to help our children understand sin. A parent may constantly teach a four or five year old child that dancing is a sin. The child may at some time start dancing to music, and then remember what the parents taught about this, and feel they have sinned. Have they? Certainly not! It is not the act that constitutes the sin, but what caused the sin—the attitude or lust.

In I Corinthians 8:4-12, Paul shows that an act may constitute sin for one person, and not for another. What is the difference? It is the understanding. To act in violation to one's conscience may constitute sin. In I Corinthians 8, Paul is discussing the eating of meat that had been offered in sacrifice to idols. Though an idol is nothing in this world, and there is only one true God, not every man has this knowledge. Some would eat these meats knowing that they had been offered to idols and some would eat the meats unknowingly. So, is it the eating of meats offered to idols that was sinful? No, it was the violation of the conscience towards that act that was sinful. In relation to this same problem, Paul wrote, *"And he that doubts is damned if he eats, because he eats not of faith: for whatsoever is not of faith is sin"* (Romans 14:23). So, an act may be a sin to some, and not to others, because of the degree of understanding.

Since repentance is a change of the mind or heart, before this change can take place it would be necessary to understand what the mind is changed from and to. How could a child change their mind about sin if they fail to understand what sin is? And, too, how could they change their mind towards God if they fail to understand some things about God? *"But without faith it is impossible to please him: for he that comes to God must believe that He is, and that He is a rewarder of them that diligently seek Him"* (Hebrews 11:6). Just as a child must be taught about God, they must likewise be taught about sin.

What if a child is baptized at too young an age to understand sin and to understand what their baptism involved? Many young people, who were baptized at a very young age realize that they did not understand what they had done, and request to be baptized again, now that they understand. It is foolish to go through life with doubts about baptism. Doubts can be erased by doing what one now has the knowledge to do. It is much better to be safe than sorry. As parents, let us teach our children, not just facts, but so they can understand about sin, God, and obedience. When they understand, they will likely respond from the heart, and not just because we have taught them facts about obedience. May God bless every concerned parent to guide their children to the Lord as early as possible.

I WANT KEVIN TO DO IT

by Larry Wishard

It is not important who baptizes my daughter. What is important is that her heart is set on giving her life to Jesus!

It had been a life changing weekend. Snow flocked the trees at Camp Eden. There had been much fun and games. Trying to whistle after eating crackers and unwrapping gum with gloves on made it a fun Fall weekend. There were the awesome sights during morning worship and the Lord's Supper. It was impossible for Spirit-filled people to look out on the unbelievable beauty of Cold Creek Canyon and not worship the Creator. On the trip back to Denver I thought that my heart was as full as it could be on November 17, 1991.

As we went to church services that night I noticed kids playing on the hillside near our church building with their snow sleds. Being very tired I just wished I could go home and take a warm city bath and rest a while. When I got to church that evening I remembered that we had a guest speaker scheduled to speak on the work in Russia. During the invitation that night a young lady, Amy Wishard, went forward. My full heart was beating very rapidly. I was totally excited. "Daddy, I want to ask Kevin to do it," she asked. "Is that okay?"

"Sure," I replied.

When the song was over, I took her confession and sent her to get ready. I prepared Kevin to baptize her. It was a beautiful end to a beautiful retreat. It did not disappoint me that she wanted a member of the youth group to do the baptizing. I was just delighted that she had chosen to give her heart to Jesus and I was going to get to live with her in heaven forever praising our Savior.

Someone asked me later if I was disappointed that she didn't ask me to baptize her. The answer was "no." We make it a practice at our church to ask the one being baptized if they have any preference. They often mention their dad or a special friend who studied with them. Sometimes they choose an elder who has been a tremendous influence over the years. This is good and has a lot of sentimental value.

But I don't believe that the one who does the actual baptizing is that important. God is the one who causes people to be baptized. Children may have good living examples around them. Parents, grandparents, uncles, aunts, and friends all have an important role to play. And out of love they may choose one of these special people to baptize them. But it is God who draws people to himself (John 6:44) and gives the increase (I Corinthians 3:7).

God gave His Son. Jesus sent the Holy Spirit to fill our hearts. Teachers and preachers over the years have kept the message going out into the world. Parents and grandparents are great influences to the children. But it seems that waiting until certain friends or relatives arrive to be baptized distorts the reality of the situation.

Jesus explained to John that the important thing was not the greatness of the baptizer, but the importance of fulfilling the righteousness of God (Matthew 3:13-15). Paul put no great emphasis on his doing the actual baptizing. He said, because of the situation, that he was glad that he baptized only Crispus and Gaius (I Corinthians 1:16). Some in Corinth were over-emphasizing the importance of the baptizer.

As we teach our children about baptism, we need to make sure that focus is not on the baptizer. Rather, focus should be on the heart of the child and the Savior.

Now an angel of the Lord said to Philip, "Go south to the road—the desert road—that goes down from Jerusalem to Gaza." So he started out, and on his way he met an Ethiopian eunuch, an important official in charge of all the treasury of Candace, queen of the Ethiopians. This man had gone to Jerusalem to worship, and on his way home was sitting in his chariot reading the book of Isaiah the prophet. The Spirit told Philip, "Go to that chariot and stay near it."

Then Philip ran up to the chariot and heard the man reading Isaiah the prophet. "Do you understand what you are reading?" Philip asked.

"How can I," he said, "unless someone explains it to me?" So he invited Philip to come up and sit with him.

The eunuch was reading this passage of Scripture: "He was led like a sheep to the slaughter, and as a lamb before his shearer is silent, so he did not open his mouth. In his humiliation he was deprived of justice. Who can speak of his descendants? For his life was taken from the earth." The eunuch asked Philip, "Tell me, please, who is the prophet talking about, himself or someone else?" The Philip began with that very passage of Scripture and told him the good news about Jesus.

As they traveled along the road, they came to some water and the eunuch said, "Look, here is water. Why shouldn't I be baptized?" And he gave orders to stop the chariot. Then Philip and the eunuch went down into the water and Philip baptized him. When they came up out of the water, the Spirit of the Lord suddenly took Philip away, and the eunuch did not see him again, but went on his way rejoicing. Philip, however, appeared at Azotus and traveled about, preaching in all the towns until he reached

38

Caesarea. (Acts 8:26-40)

Consider some of the facts of the story:

* God provided an angel to set up a meeting between a searcher and a teacher.

* God provided a portion of Scripture for them to study.

* God provided a teacher who would run to this opportunity to teach.

* God provided a Savior who was willing to pour out His blood to wash away our sins through faith.

* God provided a teacher who understood that when sin is understood and the lost person believes in Jesus as the one who takes away sin through His own blood, that is the time to be baptized.

* God provided water. When the eunuch saw the water he made a connection between Jesus, the Lamb of God, and the water baptism where he could be buried into the death of Jesus and connect with the atoning blood of the Lamb. It was not, "Look, here is water. How long before I could get the great Apostle Peter to come down to Ethiopia and baptize me?" It was not, "I want to be baptized. When will the congregation have its yearly baptism?" It was, *"Here is water. Why shouldn't I be baptized? And he gave orders to stop the chariot. Then both Philip and the Eunuch went down into the water and Philip baptized him."*

The power of baptism is not in the cherished person doing it. The power of baptism is that a sinner is being saved by Jesus who loved and died for sinners. I see this principle throughout the text. The important connection in baptism is between a person and Jesus. The denominational world has been confused, thinking that baptism is for a special audience or that it is to join a congregation.

Baptism is a response of a seeking heart to his Creator and Lord. When a person is baptized he is added to the spiritual family of God.

If there is someone special there at the time, fine. If he wants to be baptized by that special someone, fine. Don't delay your child's baptism, and don't let them delay it, simply to wait for someone to come to town. Teach them, that when it's time, we must go to the water.

Amy was baptized that day, very suddenly. She didn't wait for my approval. She responded to Jesus. Her baptism was not something between Jesus and her **and** me. It was between her and her savior, Jesus.

I didn't think the sight of Cold Creek Canyon could be outdone for glory that day. I was wrong.

STORIES OF PRESSURE

by Bob Whiddon, Jr.

In my efforts to research the subject of baptism and children, I came across many stories, both good and bad, from real life. Baptism is a beautiful thing. But sometimes things go wrong. Re-baptism happens much too often. As you read the following **true** stories, perhaps you may be helped as you lead your child to the waters of salvation. By the way, the names in these stories "were changed to protect the innocent."

Elderly Pressure

Steve was "raised in a good Christian home." They always attended church services. Steve would be the first to sign up for song leading class or Bible bowls. He was excited about the Lord and was willing to serve to the fullest of his abilities. Not bad for an eleven year old.

One day Steve's sister, who was two years older, was baptized during a morning worship. It completely surprised him since he didn't know that she was considering the act. When they left the church building that morning Steve asked his parents if he could get baptized. He felt he was just as ready as his sister was.

His parents said, "Maybe you should wait a while."

Steve's parents were good Christians. They always made time for services and fellowships of the church. But they didn't encourage prayer, Bible study, or devotionals to the Lord during the week. Steve was never discouraged, but he was never encouraged to grow in the Lord in his home.

During the next couple of years, many things changed. Steve began to notice an extreme interest in girls and sports. He spent much time in the pursuit of both. He still was active in things at the church because that's where all the girls were.

Steve's dad was asked to become an elder for the congregation. And because the congregation felt that a man needed more than one believing child per elder, Steve's dad pressed him to get baptized. But something happened over the last few years that "cooled" Steve's desire to be baptized. He wasn't against it, but it wasn't something that he was real eager for. Steve's dad didn't force the issue, but continuously talked to him about baptism.

Whenever Steve and his dad got together, Steve would be asked, "Don't you think its time?" Steve began avoiding his father and dreaded the times that he would be alone with him.

One Sunday Steve's dad called Steve into his room. "Do you think that this may be a good day to get baptized?" his father again asked. Steve was so tired of this. He told his dad "Yes" and went through the act of baptism that very morning at church.

Steve told me later that he did it "just to get dad off of my back." Not a good reason for baptism. But the story has a happy ending. Steve stayed very active in the church and was a natural leader in the youth group. It was one year, at camp, that his attitude during his baptism came back to haunt him. Steve had been teaching and baptizing some of his friends. He made sure they knew what they were doing. But then he concluded that his attitude was not right at baptism. He was baptized (re-baptized?) in the icy cold waters of a mountain stream.

Deaconly Pressure

Joe's dad was a deacon in the church. His father's duties included making sure that they had enough men for the Lord's table, prayers, ushers, etc. Joe's dad was instrumental in convincing the elders to use young, unbaptized boys in some of the duties before and after services—usually to hand out and pick up attendance cards.

Joe was very active in the church, as much as a young boy could be. He and his family were always at church. Joe would often be at the back of the auditorium welcoming guests and handing out cards.

Joe's family was much like Steve's family. They were active in fellowship and worship, but not much was said about God at home during the week. Joe knew about baptism and knew that someday he would do it, but he was not overly anxious about it.

Joe continued to be an active part of the youth group and helped with cards until he was sixteen. But then, one of the members complained about Joe. This "concerned" brother wondered if it was appropriate to have a young man take such an active part of the church if he was not baptized.

The "concerned" brother stirred up the elders who in turn talked to Joe's dad. Joe's dad began pressing Joe to get baptized, mostly because the church may make him stop ushering if he refused. Joe was confused, wondering why he had to be baptized to be an usher.

After an acceptable amount of time, and seeing that Joe's

dad could not convince Joe to get baptized, the elders told Joe that he could no longer usher at the worship services. It was shortly after this that Joe quit going to church altogether. Joe's dad could not get him to come back. It's now ten years later. Joe still has not been baptized, and has no intention to do so.

Youthful Pressure

Linda was only seven years old when she was baptized into Christ. She too came from a strong Christian home. Her family often talked about the Lord in the home.

She was a very wise young girl. She learned and remembered almost everything that she heard in Bible classes and worship services. And as a mere seven year old, she decided that she needed to be baptized. In fact, she demanded it. She tried to convince her parents to allow it. But her parents were quite concerned because of her age. They didn't think that she was old enough to be convicted of sin, to understand the Lordship of Jesus, etc.

But Linda persisted. Once she broke down in tears feeling that she was lost and needed baptism right away. Reluctantly, her parents permitted it. They were reluctant, yet confident in a way, since that little girl did demonstrate some understanding and knowledge of Scripture.

The parents worries continued even after the baptism. Their little girl was happy with her baptism, but they still wondered if she was ready. Mom and dad studied with her every night. In the next few years they all grew closer to the Lord. The family remains a strong part of a congregation today.

When Linda was about seventeen, she had decided that she was too young when she was baptized at age seven. She had studied with and baptized some of her friends and knew that baptism required knowledge and faith in Jesus Christ. She knew that a person needed to understand sin and lostness before the blood of Jesus could "save" them. She questioned her maturity at the time of her baptism. Sure, she remembered knowing a lot of things as a seven year old. But she felt she may not have had the capacity to understand back then. She told her parents of her concern and the fear that she still may be lost. Her parents took her that very hour and baptized her into Christ.

Angry Pressure

Mike was a young man who came for an unfortunate Christian home. His family was faithful in attendance to church services. But there wasn't much love in the home.

Mike's father had a problem with his image. He wanted everyone to respect him for his Christianity. But he was not a good enough Christian for anyone to respect. He would put on a good face in public, but in private he was quite mean to his wife and kids. He would threaten them so they would not misbehave in church.

Mike's older brother adjusted to his father's rage fairly well. The older brother was baptized into Christ sometime around his fourteenth birthday. It was not due to any pressure from his father. He did it to obey the Lord.

But Mike was affected by his father's anger in a different manner. Mike became rebellious, which made his father even more angry.

When Mike was fourteen his father felt that it was time for him to be baptized. But Mike refused. He just didn't see why Church and God were all that important. Obviously, they weren't that important to his father. Mike didn't want to have anything to do with empty Christianity.

The situation in Mike's home became unbearable. His

father was embarrassed in the church to have a son that was as old as fourteen and yet not a baptized member of the congregation. Mike was pressed, sometimes night and day, but refused. Eventually Mike ran away because he couldn't take the pressure.

Life for Mike's father fell apart. He couldn't handle the embarrassment and eventually fell away from the Church. His marriage fell apart within a year. Mike has never been baptized.

Ministerial Pressure

A young couple had just moved into the area. They had no friends or family—they were alone. They came into contact with a church with an energetic preacher. The preacher quickly interested them in a Bible study.

Unknowingly the preacher put a great deal of pressure upon them to get baptized. It was like the preacher was taking this couple under his wing since they were alone in town. But his zealousness caused them to shy away from him. The preacher, however, never gave up.

The couple talked together, trying to figure out what to do. They didn't want to offend their new friend, but they couldn't take the pressure. Out of desperation, they decided to be baptized so that the preacher would leave them alone. And it seemed to work. The preacher was still a good friend to them, but at least he wasn't pressing them all the time.

But the couple was concerned. They wanted to be pleasing and obedient to the Lord. And they knew that baptism to get the preacher off their back was not baptism into Jesus Christ. They wanted to be baptized again but did not want to offend their preacher friend. They wrestled with what to do for a long time. It was eating away at them.

Within a year they went home for a vacation. It was there

that they contacted the local preacher to baptize them into Jesus Christ. They were worried about their salvation. They didn't think that God would be pleased with their pressure baptism. So, they made a decision that was not based on pressure from a man, but based on love for a savior. The couple never told their preacher about their second baptism but remain friends to this day.

What Do You Think?

These stories are given for your discussion. What went wrong? What did the candidate for baptism go through? What kind of undue pressure was put upon them? What would you have changed to make them better?

Pressure is hard to see at times. As you lead your children to baptism there could be pressure place on them by you and you may not even know it. Just consider these things as you help your children in this most important time in their lives.

HOW MUCH SHOULD THE PARENT BE INVOLVED IN THE DECISION?

by Warren Wilcox

Christian parents have great concern about the souls of their own children. Because of this there is a tendency to be tremendously involved as the children reach what we consider to be the "age of accountability." A number of considerations may help in determining just how much the parents should be involved as this major decision is approaching.

First, it must be recognized that God does expect parents to raise their children within the boundaries that He has set. Many Bible passages speak to this issue.

"...bring them up in the nurture and admonition of the Lord" (Ephesians 6:4).

A widow is to be recognized for *"good works; and if she has brought up children, if she has shown hospitality to strangers..."* (I Timothy 5:10).

"Therefore, I want younger widows to get married, bear children, keep house, and give the enemy no occasion for reproach" (I Timothy 5:14).

The older women are to *"encourage the young women to love their husbands, to love their children, to be sensible, pure, workers at home, kind, being subject to their own husbands, that the work of God may not be dishonored"* (Titus 2:4-5).

The commands in these passages would certainly include making sure the children had opportunity to learn the gospel and its significance for their lives. This would include, among other things, personally teaching them, making sure they attended Bible classes and worship, and helping them to choose friends that would encourage them or, at least, not interfere with them, as they develop a lifestyle pleasing to the Lord.

When they are too young (see chapter on "Age of Accountability") to adequately understand what conversion is all about, parents would obviously have the responsibility of helping them understand. If they must be told to wait, tell them in a way that shows them that they are safe now and will need baptism later in life (see chapter on "How Do You Tell Them To Wait?")

Another consideration which must be brought up is how much of a background have they had? Not all children are "brought up in the church." On the other hand, some have attended classes and services from the time of birth. How should their background enter into parents' decisions? It will be important to determine the following:

1. How much knowledge from the Bible have they been exposed to in their lifetimes (all sources—family, friends, church)?

2. How much have they absorbed, truly understood, the things they have heard?

3. What example and emphasis have they seen at home and among their parents' friends and associates?

4. How much have they brought up their need to be

baptized and how much has it been discussed with the parents? Many parents learn about the child's decision only as the invitation song is sung and they see their child moving out of the seats into the aisle to respond. When there has been little or no part taken by the parents in such a case (especially in the younger children and young teens), and if there has been little true opportunity to learn the gospel through Bible Classes, the parents are only deceiving themselves to think that the child was truly converted.

Since it is the parents' responsibility to rear the children, it must be understood that children are responsible to the parents until they become accountable to God. Therefore, parents will be involved in helping the children determine when and if they are ready to be baptized. Some specific suggestions to aid in this area are as follows:

1. Ask them why they want to be baptized. Their answer will nearly always be a scriptural one (for forgiveness of sins, etc.) since they have heard this all their lives. However, this does not mean that they fully understand what is involved in this decision. Therefore, the parent will need to help further.

2. A straight-forward question may be necessary. **Who is the first person you think of when you do something wrong?** If their answer has to do with mom or dad, they apparently are still considering themselves in a way that would show that they have not realized the significance. They may worry more about punishment from mom and dad than disappointing God. If their answer is something like, "Well, I know what I did was against mom and dad, but I know God is displeased with it, too," then you may assume that they have begun to recognize the responsibility of their actions. Perhaps they are able to grasp the significance of obedience to God. With your help they can be guided to the point of deciding to be baptized.

3. If it is determined that they are accountable, the parents would not "push" the child nor stand in the way of his decision.

You would then bear the same relationship to his decision as you would with a neighbor or anyone you might share the gospel with. There may be more emotion involved since it is your child, but if he is to be converted, not just "dunked," he must make the decision and commitment himself.

One further word may help those who do not have an open relationship with their children when it comes to talking about spiritual things. Involve others in their study. A grandparent, uncle, friend, youth minister, preacher, elder, etc., may have a better opportunity to be directly involved in the child's decision. Your child may even feel more comfortable talking with someone else. Sometimes a child will view the parents' discussion on this matter as "something my mom and dad want me to do," rather than, "this is what I must do in order to get my life right with God."

I'm not trying to say that you should let someone else bring your child to salvation. But the fact remains that your child may, at certain points in life, appreciate the words of someone else more than you. Don't hesitate to get others to help.

Statistics from Dr. Flavil Yeakley, Jr. have appeared several times in this book already. But here are some more. Parents, be wise concerning the physical, emotional, and spiritual state of your children.

* 100% of 8 year olds baptized had either become unfaithful or had been baptized "again" because of their dissatisfaction with their earlier baptism.

* 80% of those who were baptized at 11 years old had done the same.

* 56% of those baptized at 12 years old were dropouts or were baptized again.

     * 32% of those baptized at 15 years old were dissatisfied with their original baptism.

     You are in the middle of a very important moment in your child's life. You will survive! But consider the facts as you deal with your child. Above all, pray that God will help you and your child during this time of decision.

PEER PRESSURE IN BAPTISM

by Ivy Conner

In discussing this subject the following words are defined:

PEER - "friends and family members."

PRESSURE - "influence by words or example that is
                 intended to result in changed behavior."

Therefore, when "peer pressure" is exerted it can cause
changed behavior. Peer pressure can be positive and cause
good (godly) responses; or it can be negative and cause bad
(evil) results in one's life.

Changes for good and bad, rise and fall upon
encouragement and motivation from peers. Riots and revivals
both have a sort of group dynamic of their own. If the Bible did
not speak concerning the issue of "peer pressure" we would still be
aware of its power for good or evil. We would know that good
companions help us to do right (better) and evil companions lead
us to do wrong. However, the Bible does instruct us in these areas.

BIBLE PRINCIPLES

Positive Peer Pressure

The Bible commands us to encourage one another.

*God's people in the Old Testament were constantly command to, "be of good courage" Joshua 1:6, 7, 9.

*The New Testament challenges us to exhort one another (Hebrews 10:25). That's one reason for assembling, to exhort and encourage each other.

*Barnabas exhorted the brethren (Acts 11:23).

*Judas and Silas exhorted the brethren (Acts 15:32).

*Preachers are commanded to reprove, rebuke and exhort (II Timothy 4:2).

Christian youth groups, positive activities and Christian schools encourage young people to do right.

Negative Peer Pressure

On the other hand, I Corinthians 15:33 declares that *"evil companions corrupt good morals."* We must understand the principle involved here. Negative associates often pull down, discourage and destroy spiritual interests.

*Moses warns, *"Thou shalt not follow a multitude to do evil"* (Exodus 23:2). This was obviously a negative influence of peers, leading people away from God.

*When ten spies returned from spying out the promised land and delivered a negative report to God's people, the Bible says that *"our brethren have discouraged our hearts"*

54

(Deuteronomy 1:28; Numbers 32:9).

*Hebrews 4:11 says, *"Let us therefore give diligence to enter into that rest, that no man fall after the **same example of disobedience.**"* Following a bad example is allowing a peer to influence you in a negative way.

The Message— DO NOT FOLLOW BAD EXAMPLES!

In a related issue, we need to handle the question: Should parents and friends discourage the baptisms of two or more young people at the same time? What about groups of youth being baptized during Evangelism Campaigns, Bible Camps, Vacation Bible Schools and Gospel Meetings?

Some brethren are extremely critical and outspoken on these matters and would discourage young people from responding to the Gospel in "a group." Is this a scriptural attitude? From my experience, negative pressure is often brought upon youth.

"You are not ready."
"You don't know enough."
"Wait 'till later."
"Don't be baptized just because someone else did."

Some have become discouraged and never obeyed the Gospel. Others get in with friends who have an anti-church (and even anti-Christ) attitude and are influenced to turn away from the Lord.

When two or more young people are baptized at the same time, it is often the result of the encouragement they received from each other. Such is not wrong. Let's look at some specific examples of "group" baptisms.

Bible Examples of "Group" Baptisms

The Pentecost phenomenon of Acts 2 involved group

dynamics. Think about the question, *"Men and brethren, what shall we do?"* They did not ask, *"What shall I do?"* Positive peer pressure was at work here. Peter commanded them to *"repent and be baptized everyone of you in the name of Jesus Christ for the forgiveness of your sins, and you shall receive the gift of the Holy Spirit"* (Acts 2:38). Three thousand were baptized on that day at that time, which certainly speaks of a gigantic people movement (Acts 2:41-47). Friends, family, and brethren decided to obey together.

How many of those 3,000 may have said, "If you will be baptized, then I will too" or "Let's be baptized together?" We don't know, but we do know human nature, and the psychology of people in such cases makes it likely that many did so. Was there some brother there to ask "twenty questions" about their commitment or sincerity? I think not. The scripture certainly doesn't indicate any of this type of cross-examination.

John the Baptist's ministry was to prepare people for the Lord (Matthew 3:1-17). He baptized multitudes. Could he only baptize them one at a time, or could he baptize them in large groups? The scriptures tell us of whole cities and regions who came to be baptized by him (Matthew 3:5-6).

The baptism of whole households (families) is the perfect example of peer influence to do the right thing.

*Cornelius, his household, kinsmen, and dear friends were commanded to be baptized (Acts 10:24, 27, 47-48).

*Lydia and her household were baptized (Acts 16:13-15).

*The Philippian jailer, friends, and household were baptized *"the same hour of the night"* (Acts. 16:30-34).

The Bible clearly illustrates the power of positive encouragement by peers which results in many being baptized at the same time and on the same occasion. This is positive peer pressure!

Bible Example of "Group or Peer" Re-Baptism

The account of about 12 men who were re-baptized is recorded in Acts 18:24-19:7. The apostle Paul handled this as a group conversion. Notice the use of plural pronouns: *"Ye..., ye..., they..., they..., and when they heard this they were baptized into the name of the Lord Jesus...and they were in all about 12 men"* (Acts 19:2, 5, 7). They obeyed together, yet each one had to make their own decision. Positive peer pressure plays a part in many baptisms, and negative peer pressure keeps many out of Christ.

Final Example

We are to follow in the steps of Jesus (I Peter 2:21). Although Jesus is God, He is also our peer because He is our friend (Luke 7:34; John 15:15) and brother (Mark 3:34-35; John 20:17; Hebrews 2:11). As such, His baptism is a positive "peer" pressure for us (Matthew 3:13-15, 16-17).

Conclusions

1. Baptism is an individual decision, and one must make up one's own mind. *"...whosoever will may come"* (Revelation 22:17—see also Matthew 11:28-30).

2. One must *"obey from the heart that form of doctrine"* that was taught (Romans 6:17-18).

3. Whether one obeys in a group or by one's self, it still comes down to an individual commitment between the sinner and his God. Whatever the motivation, a person must know what he is doing when he obeys Christ. There is no excuse for encouraging someone to be baptized unless they first know and understand

what they must do, and why they must do it. However, if they do know and understand, they are responsible to the Lord for their motivation, not to us. Only the Lord can know their heart.

If someone, whatever age, knows and understands the Gospel, and is convicted of their need to obey, who is to stop them from obeying their Lord? Let us encourage them as Peter did: *"And with many other words did he testify and exhort, saying, 'Save yourselves from this untoward generation.' Then they that gladly received his word were baptized: and the same day there were added unto them about 3,000 souls"* (Acts 2:40-41).

Why do we question the sincerity of two or more young people who want to be baptized together? Why do we automatically presume the youths are being unduly influenced by "peer pressure?" Wouldn't it be just as easy, and much more productive, to be positive and encourage young people (and older people and all people) to obey the Gospel at all times, once they understand the truth?

"Train up a child in the way he should go..." (Proverbs 22:6).

"Remember now thy Creator in the days of thy youth..." (Ecclesiastes 12:1).

"...by all means save some..." (I Corinthians 9:22).

"Behold, now is the day of salvation..." (II Corinthians 6:2).

The Safe Position

Many of us know young people who are moved by the love of God to obey their Lord in baptism, but some parent, preacher, or leader took it upon themselves to discourage or advise them to wait. This is very frustrating to a sincere young person, and can result in their losing interest in spiritual things. If they never return to a state of spiritual awareness, they will be lost forever. On the other hand, if they are baptized (understanding what they are doing) and later in life decide they really did not have the proper commitment, they can always be re-baptized. Encourage them always!

Let's Teach and Baptized More Youth

Once properly taught, let us encourage youth and not try to second-guess their motives. If they have not been sufficiently prepared, let us continue to teach and encourage them. Let us do our best to provide positive peer relationships, and rejoice when those relationships result in young people following the Lord!

TEACH ME WHAT I CAN DO TO HELP!

A Practical "How To" Approach in Talking with Your Children—
by Dean Bryce

"Yes, but what can I do?" the mother asked about how to handle her junior high school son who had given up the desire to go to school. The authorities had just informed her of his double life. There is no easy answer.

"Yes, but how should I handle it?" the father asked his preacher. He had just learned his 15 year old daughter's boyfriend spent last Friday night in her bedroom. How do you handle the practical matters of life?

If you have raised your child with all the benefits of Sunday school and enough preaching to teach the fundamentals of Christianity, you long for the day that your child becomes a Christian. However, when you hear the words, "Daddy, I would like to be baptized," your emotions run high! Does your baby really know enough to make this gigantic commitment? At this point, fathers and mothers must make a judgment call. The little one they used to carefully burp and diaper now wants to commit their life to the Lord Jesus. Remembering the diapers for a moment, the parent still wonders, "Does she really know enough?" How can one answer without dampening her spirits? Mothers and fathers need a strategy in ascertaining information without hindering the child's spirit.

Parents have been commissioned by God to "bring your children up in the nurture and admonition of the Lord" (Ephesians 6:4). When your child desires baptism, he or she leans upon mom and dad for advice at a vulnerable time in life.

Dad is supposed to have all the answers about bikes, cuts, and boys. Shouldn't he be informed on how to handle this most critical question which often strikes out of the blue like a lightening bolt? Where does a thunderstruck parent find practical help at such a time. To make matters worse, nothing in Scripture details exactly how to handle this situation.

Perhaps Junior's decision is correct and he should be baptized. But then again maybe he is to young and only following the lead of recent actions of other young people who have committed lives to Jesus. Possibly a brother was baptized, and his sister craves the attention he received. How do you as a parent determine the difference?

I have talked to many young people throughout the last 25 years about this delicate issue. Many parents sit nervously as I gently quiz the young believer. I'll share some things gleaned from several sources to better equip parents. This is not to drive parents away from the help of elders, preachers, and leaders, but to better equip the ones closest to the child as he makes a very important decision.

Children listen intently to my questions, weighing their answers. One may still be in elementary school, but knows exactly what he is doing. The occasion will rest firmly in the child's memory. What a teachable moment! What a great time for one to impress upon a young person at the beginning of the Christian life and the necessary holy life that follows. It is a perfect time to assist in setting reasonable expectations for the child, as he begins living this life.

Often, this special time begins with a phone call. "Preacher, Billy wants to be baptized."

"How old is he? Have you talked with him? What have you recently discussed to bring up this subject?" I inquire. They share the story. Sometimes uncertainty betrays the parent. "Do you think he knows what he is doing?" I probe.

"Would you talk to him?" they ask.

"Of course."

When I visit with the child, I usually do so away from the family, where he can stand alone. "Why do you want to be baptized?" I ask. He might say, "I want to be a better Christian" which shows he does not understand the Biblical requirements concerning baptism. I may assign him a study of the New Testament on the subject (Romans 6:1-4; I Peter 3:21; Mark 16:15-16; and John 3:3-5). I'm careful not to answer questions for him. He must come to conclusions on his own, not just repeat what others say. After this first study, we meet again.

He may answer my same question with "to obey Jesus." I ask for clarification to aid his own understanding. "How important is being baptized to you?"

Maybe he will answer, "The Bible says so." I want to know what the Bible says about it. I attentively and gently follow his reasoning. One needs to be prepared to help the child reason through his words, not as a lawyer, but as a friend.

A child saying he wants to be baptized, because he wants to become a Christian, says the right words. Probe to see what that means. I sometimes ask, "Do you have to be baptized to please God?" His answer to that question clarifies a great deal.

When the child answers, it is time to reiterate the value and meaning of their baptism. Teach them what this commitment will mean to them personally.

I inquire, "Have you sinned?" Explore what they mean by "sinned." Examples drawn from their lives illustrate whether or not they understand.

"How will your life be different after you are baptized?" takes the conversation beyond the present and towards the critical life of a dedicated disciple. Sometimes our conversations focus on the beginning of the Christian life (baptism) and fail to look further down the road. Jesus took disciples mentally down the road of discipleship by asking them to "count the cost" (Luke 14:25-33). John the Baptizer refused to immerse certain people (Luke 3:7-8) because they did not show promise for a good future life as a disciple. A study of the life of Paul (Acts 9; I Timothy 1:15-17) shows an example of changes necessary for true repentance. Quiz the child on his life and the repentance he has had. Illustrate from your own life. Put emphasis on a life committed to God, not just on the initial act of re-birth.

A most helpful exercise, in my experience, has been to ask the child to write a short letter to me as to (1) why he wants to be baptized. Look for words he uses. Terms "to be saved," "to be forgiven," and "to become a Christian" show a grasp of the importance of his decision. Also (2) how does he intend to live in the future?

The child should sign and date his letter. You should make a copy to file away. Allow him to keep his original, since this records his thinking at the time of his baptism. Sometimes young people grow up and question their knowledge at conversion, because of their youthful age. This letter, in his own handwriting, reminds him of his thoughts and provides peace of mind.

What If They Aren't Ready?

Sometimes the honest little one is simply not ready. He or she is becoming ready, but can ascertain that the child does not yet understand the entire scope of such a decision. The innocence is still there and the guilt of sin has not become clear enough.

Never discount what the child has tried to do. Compliment him and recommend that your young inquirer wait awhile. Be diplomatic and encouraging in your delay. At such times, children usually are not as crushed as much as the parents. Often the child goes skipping off to play with the other children, returning in a few months or years, understanding fully what he or she ought to do to obey Jesus.

The door should never be closed on the subject. Periodically discuss the subject in a non-threatening way, furthering the child's understanding. If a parent buries this subject until "Junior brings it up again," he may never hear the subject discussed again!

Parents Stand In The Middle

Parents teach their children how to ride a bicycle, to eat with a fork, to pray and to be responsible. Now, mom and dad stand between their child and his obedience to God. Parents want only the best for their child, but must not allow him to treat baptism in the same way as if he were joining the cub scouts. Mom and dad have the responsibility to be prepared to lead inquiring children as they make this most important decision.

HOW DO YOU TELL THEM TO WAIT—WITHOUT DISCOURAGING THEM?

by Wayne Burger

Every concerned person struggles with how to answer a young child who wants to be baptized. This is especially so if the parent or other adult has a doubt in his mind that the child needs to be baptized at this time. What do you say? How do you handle the situation so that the child won't be discouraged? You also struggle with the fact that they may be ready but you want them to wait.

When a young child asks to be baptized there needs to be a serious conversation between the parents and child with help from a preacher or elder if necessary. Even if a child responds in a public way during an invitation song, there still needs to be some talk. "It is our policy to discuss baptism with a child before we immerse them," is the way we announce it from the pulpit and in our bulletins. If some sort of policy is in place and the members are aware of it, then a child responding to an invitation won't feel like he is being singled out for further study.

The Crucial Issue

Before we even discuss the worries and concerns of a good

or bad decision to be baptized, it is crucial to let the child know this is going to be **his** decision. If you feel that he is too young or doesn't understand enough, make sure that your conversations still allow him the freedom to make his own decision.

You need to understand that if, after all the talking is over, he still wants to be baptized, I will baptize him. I may have doubts, but it is not my heart that needs to be convinced—it's his!

I may say something like, "I am so happy that you have made this decision. It's the most important decision that you will ever make. But let's talk about it. I'm not going to try to talk you out of it. This is your decision. But there are some things to think about before you are baptized."

Making sure that the child knows that it is **his** decision, his guards can be lowered and you can begin to see if the child is really ready. If not, you can lead the child to see that perhaps he needs to postpone his decision. It can be dangerous, because of his tender spiritual state, to make this decision arbitrarily for him. Our job is to help him make the right decision.

If the child leaves study saying, "They decided for me! They won't let me be baptized!" he may be so discouraged that he'll loose interest in baptism for a long, long time. Remember, it's his decision.

Vital Topics

There are three vital questions that I feel I need to ask the child before he is baptized—Why do you want to be baptized now? What is your present condition? and Do you understand the commitment involved in baptism?

First, "Why now?" The key word is "now." There are many good answers that children give like, "Because God wants me to?" But ask them, "Why now?" What happened recently to

66

make this child, somewhat out of the blue, want to be baptized?

Is it because someone else at church was baptized? We must stress to the child that baptism is an individual decision and not something done just because others are doing it. Stress the fact that just because people are the same age, does not mean that they are at the same point spiritually, emotionally, or physically.

Basically, it is a matter of maturity. It's a decision that God expect knowledgeable adults to make. Their desire to be baptized shows that children are getting closer to adult maturity. But how close is what we have to find out.

Do they want to get baptized because of the sermon that day or an especially moving devotional talk or class? Children's feelings can be touched easily. It could cause them to operate out of emotions without the proper knowledge. Find out what they have been studying in class. Perhaps you'll find out why they are rushing.

Second, "What is your present condition?" Here is where we need to get the child to see his relationship to God, sin, and to himself.

How is their relationship with God? Do they feel guilty for disobedience? Do they feel that they have been separated from God?

Do they understand what sin is? Do they know what sin does to God? There is a difference in knowing that something is wrong because mom and dad don't want them to do it and understanding what makes disobedience an act of sin. Just because they have violated their parents' wishes does not make it sin. Conviction of sin comes about by "godly sorrow" (II Corinthians 7:10). Conviction by "godly sorrow" means that they have broken God's heart by their actions. If they are not grieving over their condition and what that action has done to their relationship with God, then they may not be ready for baptism.

Third, "Do you understand the commitment involved in baptism?" Ask them what commitment means, what changes will need to be made in their life, and how they will show true commitment in their life. There has to be a willingness to demonstrate commitment. Are they ready and willing?

Perhaps they are not ready or able to make those commitments. They'll be able to see this themselves and make their own decision. We're not trying to "lay a guilt trip on them" but to help them see that if they do not see the need for change then they do not yet need to be baptized.

Methods

Are you still convinced that they are not ready for baptism? How do you tell them without discouraging them? Below are six methods or discussions that you may have with your child. You don't have to use all of them. Use whatever fits the situation.

First, let them know that just because you understand what to do does not mean that it must be done now. Commend them highly for their knowledge. Let them know how proud you are for making this decision. But then select another child, one that they know, one much younger than they are, to use as an illustration.

Ask them, "Do you think little Johnny (perhaps a five year old) could be taught to repeat the steps of salvation?" Then ask, "Do you think little Johnny needs to be baptized right now? Why not?" If they can see how immaturity will keep little Johnny from needing baptism, they might be able to see that they possibly don't need to be baptized right now either.

Second, ask them, "If you were to die tonight do you think that you would go to heaven?" If they answer yes, tell them that you believe that, too. Then explain that because they have this confidence, they do not need to be baptized.

Explain to them that children are innocent and therefore they can go to be with God without being baptized. Show them passages in which Jesus tells us to become like little children (Matthew 18:1-6). This helps the child see that God the Father and Jesus love children and that children are protected by Him. Let them know that they are already in the arms of Jesus and do not need baptism.

Third, help them realize that there are no changes necessary in their lives right now. Read and discuss passages which show that the new Christian has some changes to make (II Corinthians 5:17; Ephesians 4:22-32). Express how good you think this child is and that you see nothing in them that is so bad that they need to be baptized right now.

Fourth, discuss with them the obligations they will have as a Christian. What things would they have to stop and what things would they have to start when they are baptized? Let the child list some things that he would need to do to fulfill his obligations to the Lord. Suggest some things like better behavior in worship and classes, paying attention, applying sermons to their own lives. But, if they can't think of anything, then they are not ready.

Fifth, help the child see that this is really a decision which is to be made by those getting close to adulthood. Ask them if they are about ready to become an adult. Are they ready to put away "childish things" (I Corinthians 13:11)?

Sixth, if there is still doubt in your or your child's mind, say, "Would you like to think about it for a while?" It is good to back away from the subject for a while to get another look at it. But it can also be dangerous if nothing more is said to the child. This question, to the child, may sound more like, "I don't want you to be baptized now, so let's not talk about it anymore!"

Make sure that if you do put your child off in this way to make an appointment for sometime in the near future. Perhaps a couple of days or a couple of weeks may be sufficient. This may help the child know that his feelings are still important, and that, after those two days or two weeks, if he still wishes to be baptized, he can. Explain that it's an "adult" thing to take some time in making very important decisions.

Conclusion

Helping a child make or delay a decision to be baptized is a serious responsibility. Since we stand before God as individuals, not as families, the child must respond individually. The child will never feel discouraged as long as (1) the adults around him assure him that they will do whatever they can to make his baptism right in the eyes of the Lord, and (2) that the decision to be baptized or to delay is totally his!

We must let the children make that decision. This should be done even after going through all that we have discussed in this chapter. Even if doubt persists in our minds, we must cooperate in baptizing the child. It's their decision.

MY TEEN HAS LOST INTEREST

by Ray Wallace

The sunlight streaked low through the thick pine forest of a northeast Texas evening. It was unusually cool for May and we were enjoying the ride from Quitman to Gilmer when suddenly Dad slams on the brakes, just short of screeching the tires.

"There, look, there, in the edge of the sunlight." Dad said quietly, but excitedly as he pointed.

"What? Where?" I moved back to sight down his arm, hoping to catch a glimpse of the source of all of this hurrah. Finally one moved and I caught sight of the first whitetail deer I had ever seen.

"Look, off to the left, a buck and another doe!" Almost magically, about 12 of the tawny red coats began to take shape in broken sunlight near the edge of the clearing.

I was no more than seven, but I had learned a valuable lesson... whitetail deer are majestic, elusive, and exciting to see in the wilds! No one told me that in so many words, mind you, but the fresh breeze itself seemed alive with expectation. Dad was excited and I was hooked.

71

Twenty five years later found me in Yellowstone National Park with my wife and our grade school children. You guessed it. We stop every few minutes to photograph the deer, elk, and moose which are abundant in the park. "Are you going to save any film to take pictures of the kids?," Sandy asked, somewhat wryly. (She never really caught the germ of the "deer disease.")

And now, twelve years after the Yellowstone trip, my now married son and I venture to St. James Peak at the head of Mammoth Gulch (Colorado), cameras and binoculars in hand... expectation in our hearts. And so it goes, and so it goes.... Hand to hand, heart to heart, generation to generation *it* gets handed down. All the majestic *its* which define who we are and what life means to us. When age invades my eyes I will still see in the halls of my memory the forty inch trophy buck near the south gate of the Grand Canyon; the one which fell prey only to my Minolta. My father may not have known the finer technical points of classroom teaching, but he knew how to spread the highly communicable disease of love... love for a family, love for the outdoors, and especially love for those blasted whitetails!

And each one of you carries deep in your heart some legacy of your childhood... a hope, a dream, a love for something or someone which will keep you company to the end of your days.

The real question is "How can *you* build that special something into *your* child. More specifically, how can you build a love for Jesus into your child that will last him a lifetime? I hear the anguished cry of a thousand mothers and fathers, "My teenager has lost interest in spiritual things. When he wanted to be baptized at age 9, I encouraged him to wait, and now he seems to have lost his desire to be baptized." Or perhaps he was, indeed, baptized earlier but now has no interest in keeping his promise to God.

"What do you do? What do you say? Where do you turn?"

First, we must enumerate the major causes of loss of

interest, then deal with each one in practical ways giving practical steps to help the teen return to God.

What are the main reasons teens loose interest in Jesus? According to surveys of nearly 3,000 teens in churches of Christ from across the nation, some of the major influencers of teen morality are:

- •Closeness to parents
    - Ability to talk to parents
    - Family systems and communication
    - Focused attention from mom and dad
- •Closeness to friends
    - Types of friends teen has
    - Friends attending church youth activities
- •Teen personally attending church
- •Teen personally attending youth activities
- •Self-esteem factors

One very significant factor which surfaced in this research is that there was absolutely no statistical difference in the virginity rate between baptized and non-baptized teens. Both were just over 70 percent. That of course means that *30% of our church kids are not virgins!* I would venture to say that virginity rate would be at least one good gauge of the level of a teen's interest in spiritual things. The following statistics came from the same survey (headed by Dr. David Lewis of Abilene Christian University).

Top Five Reasons Why Teens Did <u>Not</u> Engage in Intercourse.
1. Fear of pregnancy (73%)
2. Fear of Aids (55%)
3. Because God said no (50%)
4. Wish to wait (47%)
5. Would feel guilty (39%)
      (Nearly one of five said they simply didn't have the chance!)

Top Five Reasons Why Teens <u>Did</u> Become Involved Sexually.

    1. Think they are in love (72%)
    2. Pressured into it (65%)
    3. Pleasurable (62%)
    4. To be loved (56%)
    5. Didn't think (42%)
        (42% cited low self-esteem and 35% said too much unsupervised time.)

While one might be tempted look at the overall sexual involvement rate of 30% and be glad it is at least that low, one must also examine another indicator of spirituality, the "technical chastity" rate. This rather new term is what we would have called "heavy petting" back in the 1960's. It is not merely a touch here or there, but "very heavy petting." The alarming factor is that 70% of the teens from this survey done in our churches reported that they participate in this immoral behavior. If my hypothesis is correct that sexual activity (including that which stops just short of intercourse) is an accurate indicator of spirituality, then we have a serious problem on our hands.

It may surprise many to learn that factors cited in these survey results which had the strongest influence on teen morality (and thus the battle for spirituality itself) are supportive parents who are *both baptized*, exhibit understanding attitudes, and encourage their children to make their own decisions. Many have formerly thought that "scaring hell" out of their children with hell-fire and brimstones pronouncements was the best approach. Whether it ever was may be debatable. With today's kids in today's world, however it is becoming increasingly obvious that love is the key. Maybe, just maybe, Jesus was right after all when He said, *"If you love me, you will keep my commandments"* (John 14:15).

I am not a "change agent church basher" but it is my honest opinion that many of our churches have done a wonderful job teaching points of doctrine or debate, but have done a woefully lacking job of teaching our kids to love Jesus. But guess what? God never intended it to be the *church's* responsibility to teach your children to love Jesus. Never in the scriptures is there found any injunction to the church to teach your children to follow Jesus or to love Him. That is the exclusive domain of parents in God's scheme of things.

So what can you do as a parent?

First, let's look at the practical approach. Examine the major factors listed earlier in this chapter. Xerox the page and put it in your Bible (your kids will never look there!). Begin to spend time, real time, listening time with each of your children, individually. Focus on that family closeness by pursuing hobbies together, making trips together, and definitely making visits to elderly church members with your kids. Allow them to communicate their feeling, fears, frustration. Listen reflectively, "That must be very frustrating" or "That would bother me, how does it make you feel?"

Begin to monitor their friendships more carefully. *"Do not be deceived, bad company corrupts good morals"* (I Corinthians 15:33). Stop believing that just because your little angel has been baptized that he or she is not going to become like the people they "hang with." They indeed will, and if you believe otherwise you are not only being naive but also "deceived."

The battle to rekindle your teen's interest in Jesus must not be under- estimated. Satan, himself, is your adversary! The battle calls for a major weapon of time. **You must buy up your teen's time!** Plan more things for the two of you or for the family, **and make it fun!** Hiking trips, biking trips, camping trips, hobby shops, model planes, model cars (okay, real cars), ball games, hunting, and fishing, are only a few of the possibilities. **Buy up their time!** I have not met a teenager yet who does not love time with mom or dad **if it is done right. Listen to them, learn from**

them. Listen long enough to examine their culture *and yours* through their eyes. If something doesn't make sense, ask them to explain it. Eventually, they will get the idea that it is okay to ask you to explain something the older culture they have never understood.

But honestly, that is the easy part.

The second and harder part in winning your teen's interest back to "spiritual things" is the change that *usually* must take place in *you,* the parent.

In working with a congregation in Dallas for several years, one fact became quite evident. There are three levels of teens.

1. Involved, spiritual, God-loving teens who become leaders. Their parents are the ones who love Jesus and the church, and are involved, with love and interest in their hearts and daily lives.

2. The "middle group" - teens who are somewhat involved, attend a fair number of the youth activities, attend services most of the time, but seem to struggle more in their personal faith and involvement. Their parents are usually not Christians and seldom or never come. These teens were brought by friends in the first group, and are "learning the ropes" of commitment.

3. The "problems" - kids who are a constant challenge. No not just a "cut-up" but one who causes real trouble. The ones you really can't trust, especially alone with the opposite sex. The parents of these kids are the uninvolved SMO's (that's Sunday Morning Only). The parents are not mean or hateful, they just don't really get involved with Jesus and His work on earth. They don't do a lot of bad things, in fact they don't do much at all. But the one thing that usually marks this family is that the parents (especially the father) demands a much higher degree of submission to his authority than he (father) has toward God.

You as a parent must "catch the germ." You, as a person, must examine you individual commitment to Jesus. Stop using the term "spiritual things!" God never commanded us to love "spiritual things." God gave us an older brother to love, not a thing!!!

[I know, I know, I've started preaching, but bear with me... someone's eternity may be at stake.]

Catch the "germ" dad. Catch the "germ" mom. I don't mean to *act* like you love Jesus so your kids will love Him. They will see through you like crystal! No one will know you better than your kids. They live with you and they are not as benevolent in their assessments as your wife may be! Kids are brutally honest, on the playground and at home. One young, long-haired teen refused to work. When asked why he simply said, "Dad, for years I have seen that the most important thing in your life is planning for retirement. I agree with you that it must be the most important thing in life, and I have simply beaten you to it!"

Catch the germ. Slam on the brakes when you pass a Bible bookstore and take the kids in to browse. Be excited. Be genuine. God and His work are profoundly exciting! **Point to the deer at the waterbrook of Psalm 42:1!**

"Can you see it son, in your mind's eye. Perhaps he was chased by a lion and barely escaped! Tell me what you see the deer doing there, tired and hot by the waterbrook. Drinking? Right? How badly does he want that water? Do you think he wanted it as badly as you did yesterday when we hiked to timberline? Remember how our throats were sticking together, so dry and hot? That's the way the deer is. And that's the way my heart yearns for God. Let's set here awhile and let Jesus talk to us from the Sermon on the mount. I know, you read 5 verses and I'll read 5 verses. You go first, I love to hear you read the words of Jesus. Wow, that's neat. Just think, you and I are hungering and thirsting for Jesus, just like that deer... just like here, in Matthew 5:6. Won't it be super to see Jesus, to meet Him in person and hug his neck. Look, over there, a mule deer by the stream at the edge

77

of the light coming through the trees.... And look, a buck and another doe."

Catch the germ. I believe that few children learn to love Jesus more than their mom or dad loves him. And how is love shown? Sacrifice! Time, money, interest, excitement, consistency.

Model it dad. Model it mom. Remember, my dad never once even hinted **verbally** that I should love deer hunting or the outdoors in general. Never once did he debate the finer points of sneaking up on trout in a clear beaver pond. He just lived it.

Catch the germ and pass it on. Read Deuteronomy 6... slowly, more carefully than ever. And when your son asks you in time to come saying, "What do the testimonies and the statutes and the judgments mean which the Lord commanded you?" then you shall say to your son.... And you tell the story of how God rescued the people from Egypt. I know, I know... you may feel a bit awkward at first, but tell the story of the ten plagues, the Red Sea, Goliath, etc. and tell them with fire in your eyes... tell them in play by play fashion like you told of the Bronco game at the water cooler at work today. Tell them with all the excitement I saw in my father when whitetails were near. Make it real. Make it a part of your own life.

Two last admonitions: The path you start will be the ones your children finish; and, whatever you excuse in moderation, your children will abuse in excess.

Do you feel like it is too late? Get on your knees with that child tonight and beg his forgiveness for not loving Jesus more all *his* life! Ask *him* or *her* to pray for you... and I will be too. May God bless your efforts to love Him more and to lead your children into His paths.

I must end here. I am going home to pack for tomorrow. Ralph and Shane and I are leaving early to scout out Mammoth

Gulch for the coming deer season. I know, I'm hopeless, just blame my Dad!

WHAT IF IT WAS TOO SOON?

by Ron Carter

I have memories of a mother who came to me to discuss the fact that her ten-year-old son wanted to be baptized. "I'm not sure I'm ready for this," she said. Puzzled, I asked what she meant by that. Her answer had nothing to do with the spiritual maturity of the child or the lack of it. Her concern was about her being prepared to accept his maturity simply because it meant she would have to come to terms with the fact that she was getting older. Without realizing it, she was allowing her own emotions to take priority over the spiritual welfare of her child. This is just one example of how parents can lose track of their real purpose. Selfishness comes in many deceptive forms.

So what should parents do when they are faced with a child who wants to be baptized? The first thing I want to acknowledge is that the answers are much easier to write down than to have the wisdom to put them in practice. But the fact that it is difficult should cause us to realize just how important it is for parents to prepare for this moment before the fact. To be caught off guard can cause even the wisest of parents to mishandle a situation as they try to play catch-up. Preventive medicine is always best. Parents, do not wait until your child approaches you about this subject before you consider what your response will be. Fathers and mothers who have made spiritual training an ongoing process from the moment of the child's birth will have a much easier time handling the occasion.

Our common purpose is to do God's will and to teach our children to do the same. Paul expanded on this in Ephesians. *"Blessed be the God and Father of our Lord Jesus Christ, who has blessed us with every spiritual blessing in the heavenly places in Christ, just as He chose us in Him before the foundation of the world, that we should be holy and blameless before Him, in love,"* (1:3-4). We are here to prepare for that time when we will all stand before God. That is our Eternal Purpose. With these things in mind, let us continue our search with the pleasure of God as our primary motivation.

"But seek first His kingdom and His righteousness; and all these things shall be added to you," (Matthew 6:33). Since we want to end up with children who are faithful, putting God first in their lives, possibly a chain-of-command approach would help us to see more clearly. Paul left no doubt that obedience is the first thing children need to learn. *"Children, obey your parents in the Lord, for this is right. Honor your Father and mother which is the first commandment with a promise, that it may be well with you, and that you may live long on the earth"* (Ephesians 6:1-3). Notice that obedience to parents is conditional in the words *"in the Lord."* This is emphasized again in the following verse when he said, *"And, fathers, do not provoke your children to anger; but bring them up in the discipline and instruction of the Lord."*

Although obedience to parents is obviously important, as part of God's plan, obedience to God is primary. Therefore, in the Christian home, the chain of command is God first and parents second. In the church and in society, the chain may vary slightly. No matter what the case, however, obedience to God always takes precedence.

If parents have done a good job of training their children for unwavering allegiance to God, when the time comes for them to consider baptism, it will take its place as just one more act involved in the natural sequence of events in the child's spiritual growth. All things being equal, I do not believe that parents have the right to tell their children that they can or cannot be baptized. This is finally between them and God—a personal matter. Certainly, parents do have the responsibility to make certain that the child's action is not based on frivolous thinking. Once again, it depends on the previous training of the child. The child who has been trained well will understand that this decision is between them and God.

I would simply say to the child that this is one time when parents can only serve as advisors. If the child is truly concerned about meeting the conditions God has established for our salvation, isn't a parent violating the "God first" principle by denying the child the opportunity to be obedient to those conditions?

No matter what the age of the individual might be, there are certain prerequisites in regard to baptism. These were established very clearly on the day of Pentecost. Peter's answer to the question, *"What must I do?"* was *"Repent, and let each of you be baptized in the name of Jesus Christ for the forgiveness of your sins; and you shall receive the gift of the Holy Spirit"* (Acts 2:38). This, of course, requires that the individual acknowledge sin in their life and that this sin must be taken away by obedience to God's plan. A person who has repented of their sins, and has been baptized so that those sins will be taken away, has done what is necessary to become part of the Body. To suggest that a baptism is not valid because the individual was not knowledgeable of everything a Christian life needs to be, is to say more than the Bible says. Age has absolutely nothing to do with it.

Is it possible for a person to go down into the water for the wrong reason? Of course it is. But that can happen at any age. A child may want to be baptized simply because several other children of the same age group have recently done the same. Or he may want to do it because he wants to take the Lord's Supper.

However, there are also adults who say they want to be baptized when their real motivation is simply that they want to marry a person who won't marry them otherwise.

If baptism is done for the wrong reason, it is not baptism. This is why it is a mistake to use the term "rebaptism." Technically there is no such thing. If a person goes down into the water, motivated by something other than what Peter was talking about, that person has not been baptized. No matter what the baptizer says at that moment, no matter whether the congregation puts their name in the church directory, that person is not part of the Body of Christ.

What if it was too soon? What if the child really wasn't ready? To answer this to the satisfaction of everyone will require that I set aside some of my basic beliefs in parenting. I believe that parents who are on top of all aspects of their children's training, who are truly involved in their children's lives, will know if their child is ready even before the child brings it up. They will not be surprised by the child's interest.

For the sake of the situation where there may still be some question about it being too soon, allow me to pose a question. So what if it were to happen too soon? As the years go by, and the child continues to be trained in all of the Christian principles, the power of truth will eventually cause that individual to realize that the action they took was not really baptism. When that happens, They simply need to be encouraged to do what they need to do. We need to get it out of our heads that God is somehow going to place a black mark beside the name of that child, or the parent involved, when the response is proven to have been too soon.

I believe there are many people who go through the act of baptism again simply because they can't remember what was on their minds when they made their decision. "Did I do it for the right reason?" There are also those who are struggling to come to terms with just how much they didn't know when they were baptized. Not realizing just how simple the prerequisites really are, they feel the need to do it again. Many times this is done when all that is really necessary is repentance.

When someone does come to me expressing doubt about the validity of their baptism, my response is always the same. I first ask them what they do remember about why they were baptized and then I go on from there. Even then I always tell them, "If you still have any doubt about your position, there is only one way to get rid of that doubt. Take care of it by being baptized." Notice I said "baptized" not "re baptized." God is certainly not going to penalize someone for going through this act twice, even if they did it for all the right reasons the first time.

Finally, I want to share two ideas that may be of some help in the decisions parents must make in this regard. For the past several years, when I am involved in someone's baptism, I ask them to sit down that very day and write themselves a letter. In this letter I ask them to express exactly how they feel and why they took this action. If that person is ten, twelve, fifteen or even fifty, the time may come when their memory of what motivated them will fade and this letter will help to refresh that memory.

The other idea is also vital to our subject. Parents need to think about every aspect of the situation. It would be so much better for them to take the chance that the child might be taking this action too soon, than to deny them and somehow take away the sense of urgency of this action. I have memories of parents who would not allow their children to be baptized and then lived to regret it because these same children never became Christians. It all comes down to an examination of both alternatives. If the parents say no, what are the possible consequences? If they allow it, what is the worst that can happen?

Once again, we need to emphasize the importance of not waiting until the subject comes up before parents think about the way they will handle it. If we are fulfilling our God-given responsibilities as parents, the baptism of our children will be a time of joy rather than of dilemma. It will simply be one of the blessings that come from the seeds we have sown in our efforts to train our children and to *"...bring them up in the discipline and instruction of the Lord."*

ORDER FORM

I would like to order additional copies of
From Children to Brethren

_____ Books ($6.95 each)   _____

                          Sub-total   _____
                          Shipping*   _____
                          Tax**   _____
                          Total   _____

[ ] Check or money order enclosed   [ ] Visa   [ ] Master Card

Card #:_____ Exp. Date:_____

Signature:_____

Ship to:_____

Address_____

City_____ State_____ Zip_____

*Add $2 shipping for each book
**Colorado residents add 3.8% sales tax

SEND YOUR ORDER TO:

S.U.N. PUBLISHING
P.O. Box 381
Westminster, CO 80030

OR CALL: (303) 753-2915 and leave order with your Master
Card/Visa name, number, and date.